SECRET INDIANA

A Guide to the Weird, Wonderful, and Obscure

Jamie Ward

REEDY PRESS

Reedy Press
PO Box 5131
St. Louis, MO 63139
reedypress.com

Library of Congress Control Number: 2024948753
ISBN: 9781681065847

Design by Jill Halpin

Unless otherwise indicated, all photos are courtesy of the author or in the public domain.

We (the publisher and the author) have done our best to provide the most accurate information available when this book was completed. However, we make no warranty, guarantee, or promise about the accuracy, completeness, or currency of the information provided, and we expressly disclaim all warranties, express or implied. Please note that attractions, company names, addresses, websites, and phone numbers are subject to change or closure, and this is outside of our control. We are not responsible for any loss, damage, injury, or inconvenience that may occur due to the use of this book. When exploring new destinations, please do your homework before you go. You are responsible for your own safety and health when using this book.

Printed in the United States of America
26 27 28 29 5 4 3 2

CONTENTS

God's Garden

ACKNOWLEDGMENTS

Throughout the year of writing this book, I encountered numerous obstacles. However, the unwavering support of my closest friends, family, and church gave me the confidence to begin and complete this project. Despite life's difficulties, my passion for travel and writing has remained unwavering, and I am determined to continue pursuing my heart's desires through the discovery and documentation of these narratives.

My daughters, Lela and Faith, both born and raised in Indiana, are significant sources of my inspiration. Even though they are now adults, some of my most cherished memories involve the three of us taking spontaneous road trips during school breaks and our "Starbucks Saturdays." They will always hold a special place in my heart, and I love them dearly.

I want to thank the Midwest Travel Network and my community of fellow travel writers for their mentorship, friendship, and encouragement.

Finally, I extend my deepest gratitude to my devoted readers, who consistently read my blog, engage on social media, and support me by purchasing my books. Without your unwavering dedication, my writing journey would not be possible.

Holliday Park

INTRODUCTION

While reading this book, you may wonder why I didn't include many other intriguing locations in Indiana deemed *Secret Indiana* worthy. I wish I could have! The reality is that while the state is brimming with remarkable places, fitting them all into a single book is a herculean task. As a lifelong Hoosier, I continue to stumble upon new hidden gems and "secrets" throughout the state. My travels often lead me to small towns, where I uncover the most unusual places. This book has oddities, hidden treasures, peculiar destinations, folklore, and sites and structures with legendary and eerie tales.

Crafting these pages and writing the stories was an exhilarating adventure for me. Discovering something previously unknown always excites me, and I can't wait to share these discoveries with others. Within these pages are everything from artesian springs to hair-rising tales of haunted buildings and historical hidden gems. These are just a few of the many treasures that you'll find in this book. If you seek something fun, historical, or weird, you'll find it here.

So whether you're a lifelong Hoosier or just visiting the state for the first time, I encourage you to explore these secret Indiana spots and discover the magic beyond the beaten path.

For more Indiana discoveries, my book *100 Things to Do in Indiana Before You Die* highlights the top hundred experiences within the state. You can also explore more through my travel articles online at fieldsandheels.com or on social media @fieldsandheels.

AN OPEN-AIR UTOPIAN SANCTUARY

What is the significance of a church without a roof?

The 1800s utopian village of New Harmony is peaceful and uniquely charming. Inside the walkable town, visitors can explore the Jane Blaffer Owen Sanctuary (JBO Sanctuary), an open-air site featuring gardens, fountains, sculptures, architecture, and the unique Roofless Church. This outdoor private art collection, founded by Jane Blaffer Owen, is open to the public and showcases Owen's dedication to preserving the historic utopian legacy of New Harmony's spiritual and creative expression.

In 1957, Owen commissioned famous architect Philip Johnson to design the Roofless Church, which is not an actual building but rather an expansive plaza featuring a cathedral, spire, flanking gardens, sculptures, and an overlook. The unique open-air cathedral is encapsulated by 12-foot-high walls and a grand golden gate designed by the acclaimed artist Jacques Lipchitz. Within the sanctuary-like walls are six sacred spaces, each offering a unique tribute to meditation.

JANE BLAFFER OWEN SANCTUARY

WHAT: An open-air spiritual sanctuary with gardens and art

WHERE: 420 North St., New Harmony

COST: Free

PRO TIP: Visit JBO Sanctuary year-round for self-paced tours from dusk to dawn.

The JBO Sanctuary offers four overnight spaces for creatives, artists, writers, scholars, and JBO Fellows to get away and retreat. The Sanctuary provides extended stays for up to two weeks.

Right inset: *The Roofless Church inside the Jane Blaffer Owen Sanctuary.*

The purpose of this architectural wonder is to welcome individuals of all faiths to worship together, acknowledging that the sky is the only roof vast enough to encompass a diverse congregation. The Roofless Church's design was inspired by Divine Proportion, a centuries-old method that artists and designers have utilized based on the patterns found in nature. During my last visit, I sat in serene tranquility, surrounded by the peaceful sounds of birds and nature.

Owen also helped install the Cathedral Labyrinth, a place for meditation and prayer. Located just a short walk from the JBO Sanctuary, the labyrinth offers another peaceful site for relaxation, rest, and solitude.

A LIBRARY WITH SECRETS WITHIN THE BOOKS

Why are there notes hidden in the West Baden library?

Nestled within the French Lick Resort, the West Baden Springs Hotel is a testament to history and luxury. Built in 1902, this iconic hotel is one of three at the resort. Its grand atmosphere and Old World charm have attracted renowned individuals for over a century. Guests are captivated by the 200-foot-diameter atrium and colossal fireplace that greet them.

During my stay at West Baden Springs, I was drawn to the hotel's library and its collection of books. Surprisingly, I discovered notes and letters tucked away in some of them. Upon inquiry, I learned that a unique tradition has emerged among the guests since 2012: hiding notes in the library's books.

Initially discovered by a hotel employee in classic novels, this practice has flourished over the years. Guests have continued leaving notes or adding or replying to previously left ones. These notes have become a part of the resort's history, serving as a time capsule that captures the experiences and thoughts of visitors.

During your visit, open any book to read the handwritten letters left behind by previous visitors. These letters include love letters, exchanges, secret confessions, memories, treasure hunts,

---

The Late Night Jazz Club plays live jazz music in the library every Friday and Saturday night from 9 p.m. to midnight.

WEST BADEN SPRINGS HOTEL LIBRARY

WHAT: A historic hotel library with hidden notes and letters

WHERE: 8538 West Baden Ave., Baden Springs

COST: Free

PRO TIP: The French Lick Resort is open to the public but may be closed during private events.

and notes. However, be mindful when children are reading the letters, as some may contain steamy content. If you're feeling adventurous, leave your note for future visitors. And if you're lucky, you can find the handwritten note I left!

OTIS THE SASQUATCH

Where can you catch a sighting of Bigfoot?

If you've never had the pleasure of encountering a friendly sasquatch, Otis is a must-see. In southern Indiana, you'll find a majestic 25-foot-tall Bigfoot sculpture named Otis, crafted by the skilled hands of Bear Hollow Wood Carvers. This impressive wooden artwork took five days and the dedication of nine carvers to bring to life. Among all the Bigfoot sculptures I've encountered, Otis remains the largest. Shaggy and towering, he emanates a sense of gentle camaraderie with his inviting facial expression.

At the French Lick Cabins at Patoka Lake Village, Otis is a popular attraction that draws visitors to the region. Inspired by the Otis Redding song "(Sittin' On) The Dock of the Bay," the carving depicts Otis sitting on a bowing fishing dock, holding a fishing pole. Locally sourced materials were used to create this work of art: sawmill slabs from Paoli Bender Lumber were used for the fur, while solid white pine logs were used for the face and feet.

Otis can be found at the entrance of Patoka Lake Village, and his enormous size makes him impossible to miss. Despite attempts to keep him a secret until his completion in 2023, visitors to the cabins and the area have been enthusiastically taking selfies and photos in front of him, making him an Internet sensation.

OTIS AT PATOKA LAKE VILLAGE

WHAT: A 24-foot wooden Bigfoot carving

WHERE: 7900 W Co. Rd. 1025 S, French Lick

COST: Free

PRO TIP: In French Lick, you can visit the Bear Hollow retail store, the carvers who created Otis.

Otis greets visitors at the entrance of Patoka Lake Village.

Reports of sasquatch sightings in Indiana have emerged, accompanied by photographic evidence. However, fear not, as the mystery creature in question is none other than the amiable Otis.

A TASTE FROM OUTER SPACE

Why is Yoda hanging out at this restaurant?

Lady Tron's is a unique dining destination inside an authentic 1956 Valentine portable steel diner, with a distinct sci-fi theme. Valentine diners, known for their capacity of 8 to 10 seats, were conceived during the challenging times of the Great Depression, and only a limited number remain in operation.

This diner is a must-visit for those who appreciate hearty soups, delicious sandwiches, and an immersive retro atmosphere inspired by outer space. The owner's lifelong fascination with science fiction originated in her childhood, as her father made it a tradition to watch *Star Trek* every Sunday after church.

LADY TRON'S

WHAT: A sci-fi diner

WHERE: 147 E Market St., New Albany

COST: Varies based on menu prices

PRO TIP: Seating is limited, but carryout is available, and there is outdoor seating if you visit in the warmer months.

Photo courtesy of SoIN Tourism

Upon entering the restaurant, you might find yourself transported into an episode of *Star Trek*. You are greeted by a ceiling adorned with cosmic spray-painted art and recognizable pop culture characters such as Yoda, the Jetsons, and E. T. Space-themed characters and artwork can be found inside and outside the establishment. Many of the decorative items were gifted by the regulars of Lady Tron's. The eatery can accommodate up to 10 people, and outdoor seating is available during warmer months.

Lady Tron's also offers an "out-of-this-world" menu, complementing its unique ambiance. Among the quirky themed entrees, you'll find the Riply, a pulled chicken sandwich with blueberry molasses, and the Leia, a sweet grilled cheese with apple butter. The restaurant's handwritten menu is updated daily, showcasing specials and additional offerings.

Photos courtesy of SoIN Tourism

Lady Tron's diner exterior resembles a spaceship, and a metal robot welcomes guests at the entrance.

THE OFFICIAL TRAIN ROBBERS

How does the legacy of the infamous Reno gang end?

In 1866, the notorious Reno gang, led by brothers Frank, William, and Simeon Reno, committed the world's first train robbery in Seymour, Indiana. Disguising themselves as passengers, they boarded the train as it departed Seymour's depot and successfully robbed the occupants of $16,000. They managed to evade capture initially.

However, the Reno gang's reign of terror did not end there. Before the Seymour robbery, they had already pulled off several daring escapades and gotten away with them. Their luck held for three years following the Seymour heist, during which time they continued to commit train robberies and elude capture.

In 1868, while a train passed through Seymour, three members of the Reno gang (not the brothers) were apprehended by vigilantes. The men were hanged and buried right there on the spot, a location known as the "Hangman Cross." Later that year, the Reno brothers were finally captured and sent to a well-guarded prison in New Albany to avoid another vigilante attack. However, this did not deter the Scarlet Mark Society, a large vigilante group. One hundred of them raided the prison, broke into the brothers' cell, and promptly lynched them.

The Reno brothers were buried together in Seymour, the location of their first significant crime. Their gravesites can be found in Seymour's Old City Cemetery, surrounded by a fence to maintain a respectful distance for tourists. A plaque describing the graves is positioned at the beginning of a small, cemented pathway leading to the simple graves.

GRAVES OF THE RENO GANG

WHAT: The lynching and grave site of America's first train robbers

WHERE: Old City Cemetery, E 9th St., Seymour

COST: Free

PRO TIP: The graves, enclosed by a small fence, are closest to Shields Avenue. Hangman's Crossing is about 2.5 miles west of town at a railroad crossing along US Hwy. 50.

A pathway and plaque guide visitors to the burial site of the Reno Three.

Although the deaths of the Reno brothers effectively ended the Reno gang, numerous copycat gangs emerged across the country, culminating in the era known as the Wild West.

A PIONEER'S LEGACY

How did this historic gristmill evolve over the centuries?

Beck's Mill was constructed in 1808 by George and Betsy Beck, pioneers among the early settlers. This historic gristmill initially measured a modest 15 by 15 feet and was built from sturdy stones and logs. Later that same year, a sawmill was added to the complex, further expanding the mill's capabilities.

Due to its growing success, the original mill was replaced by a larger structure in 1820. However, disaster struck in 1864 when a fire destroyed it. Beck's son rebuilt the mill, preserving its legacy. During this reconstruction, carding machines and a wool-picker were installed on the second floor, enhancing the mill.

Just across the road, approximately 165 feet away, a fort was constructed, leaving behind a cornerstone that remains visible. Beck developed Indiana's second-largest spring, which emerges from a mile-long cave in the bluff behind the mill site. This spring provided water power for his mill, as well as his log cabin and stone mill. Beck's Cabin, in the

BECK'S MILL

WHAT: A historic gristmill

WHERE: 4433 S Becks Mill Rd., Salem

COST: Fee for admission

PRO TIP: Cash or check is the only accepted form of admission payment. Verify the operating hours before your visit, as the mill may close due to high water levels or extreme heat.

Beck's Mill became a significant resource for the community in the 18th century, attracting numerous settlers. Today, it is a landmark for an industry that shaped Salem's history.

woods above Historic Beck's Mill, was assembled on the same site as George Beck's original homestead. The original cabin, however, collapsed due to neglect.

The modern roller mills of the late 19th century, combined with the growth of urban areas, ceased operations at Beck's Mill in 1914. It remained idle and deteriorated for 50 years until it underwent a restoration project in 2008, returning it to operational condition. Today, volunteers operate the mill, which was added to the National Register of Historic Places in 2007. It is the last extant mill in Indiana that uses only grindstone milling throughout its entire process.

The mill's site is unique in that it is one of the highest elevations in Indiana, at 946 feet above sea level. It is situated in a rocky ravine surrounded by trees.

SHADE FOR INDIANA'S FOUNDING FATHERS

CONSTITUTION ELM

WHAT: A historic landmark where Indiana's first constitution was written

WHERE: 200 W High St., Corydon

COST: Free

PRO TIP: For a self-guided historic walking tour, begin at the Harrison County Visitor Center to pick up a map of the area's significant sites.

Under which tree was Indiana's first constitution written?

In the absence of air-conditioning in 1816, the delegates drafting Indiana's first constitution sought relief from the sweltering heat of a June day. They gathered beneath the shade of a large elm tree, the largest tree located outside the first capitol building, a humble log cabin pending the completion of the permanent statehouse. This majestic elm, stretching over 130 feet across and reaching a height of 50 feet, provided ample shade for the 43 men in attendance.

It was common for delegates to seek refuge under the shade of a tree, particularly during the warm summer months. This particular tree, later known as the Constitution Elm, holds significant historical importance. Efforts were made to preserve the tree, but unfortunately, it succumbed to the Dutch Elm disease in 1925.

In Indianapolis, the Indiana Statehouse displays the 1816 Constitution, housed within a wooden enclosure crafted from the historic Constitution Elm tree.

To honor its legacy, the tree trunk was preserved with coal tar and surrounded by a large sandstone monument, making it known as the Constitution Elm Stump. Additionally, pieces of the tree's wood were carefully preserved and transformed into souvenirs and other commemorative items, ensuring that a piece of this historic tree continues to live on.

A BOOKSTORE WITH A SECRET TUNNEL

Why are there secret passages under this bookstore?

In 2021, brothers Sam and Adam Morris made a startling discovery while renovating their newly acquired bookstore in downtown Evansville. During renovations, they stumbled upon a hidden tunnel beneath the business. Before opening the bookstore, they stripped the building down to its concrete foundation for renovations. In the process, they uncovered a concealed door leading to a hidden room beneath the floor. Upon lifting the door, they were astounded to find a hole in the floor leading to a small 10x10 brick room. Intriguingly, there was a hole in the wall of this room, which initially led them to believe it was just an old basement connected to a neighboring basement.

The hidden room captured the attention of the Evansville African American Museum, sparking speculation that it might hold clues about the Underground Railroad. With the help of a $50,000 grant, the museum engaged an archaeologist who uncovered that the tunnels were remnants of Prohibition-era passages beneath Main Street.

Evidence of the 1937 flood in Evansville remains visible in the two feet of silt accumulated within the tunnels. Artifacts discovered include still parts, glass bottles, and a built-in table and chair, suggesting the possible existence of a gambling den. The tunnels end where a four-story building at 420 Main once stood. While Evansville's Prohibition history is

---

Looking for an interesting, unique, or banned book? You'll find it here! The bookstore also frequently has poetry nights and book signings.

YOUR BROTHER'S BOOKSTORE

WHAT: Secret Prohibition rooms and tunnels under a bookstore

WHERE: 504 Main St., Evansville

COST: Free to visit, varies based on purchases

PRO TIP: The tunnel isn't publicly open, but ask Adam or Sam about it and its history—they'll show you to the trapdoor (part of the bookstore floor) and tell you the story!

well-documented, the history of this building remains a mystery. Records date back to 1919, but its earlier purpose has yet to be discovered. It has been linked to mobsters, a Chinese syndicate involved in the distribution of ancient Chinese medicines, and it was a dance studio.

Although the tunnels are still being explored, excavations require an archaeologist. Evansville became a prime location for alcohol smuggling across the river when Indiana was a dry state, so it makes sense that Prohibition tunnels are present in Evansville. In the future, the bookstore owners plan to establish a small museum about the tunnels in their store.

If you'd like to discover more about the tunnels or Evansville's Prohibition history, consider visiting Your Brother's Bookstore.

THE GREY LADY IN THE LIBRARY

Why are there Ghost Cams in Indiana's oldest library?

The breathtaking Willard Library is a Victorian Gothic architectural marvel built in 1881. It is the oldest public library in the state and was initially built to be a college. However, due to insufficient funding and economic challenges, founder Willard Carpenter transformed his dream into a library where the community could learn and grow.

Before the library's construction was completed and its doors could open in 1885, Willard passed away in 1883. Because Willard donated his entire inheritance to public charity, the library served as a bitter reminder to his family that he valued the city more than them.

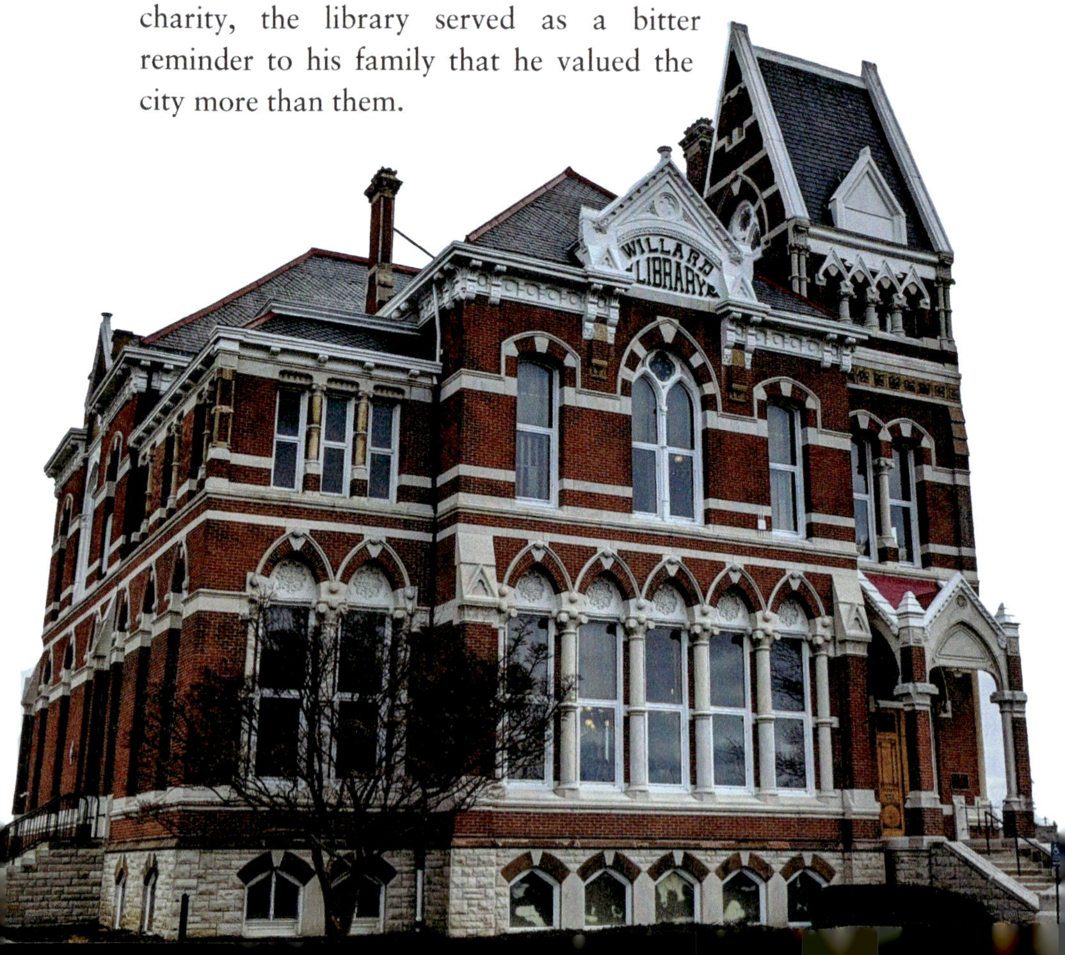

One of the Ghost Cams is in the library's stairwell. Witnesses have reported seeing a female figure garbed in a graceful, flowing dress, her presence enhanced by a ghostly, ethereal gray veil.

WILLARD LIBRARY

WHAT: An 1885 historic library in a "haunted" Victorian Gothic building

WHERE: 21 N 1st Ave., Evansville

COST: Free

PRO TIP: To schedule a tour, email willard@willard.lib.in.us or call 812-425-4309 in advance.

Half a century after the library opened, a custodian encountered a ghostly presence that prompted him to quit his job. Since then, numerous sightings of a ghost, dubbed "the Grey Lady," have been reported. Legends suggest that the ghost is Louise, Willard's daughter, who still harbors unresolved grievances and continues to haunt the library's patrons. The frequency of these sightings has led to the installation of six Ghost Cams, allowing the public to watch for any paranormal activity around the clock through online streaming.

The Grey Lady was last spotted in 2010 in the basement hallway and is said to have a musky perfume scent. Library staff, police officers, visiting lecturers, a local weathercaster, and patrons have all seen her. The ghost is said to move books and furniture, turn water on and off, and make noises. Some people have also reported feeling cold or having their hair or earrings touched in her presence.

During the day, the Willard Library appears to be a typical library. However, you can attend one of its popular ghost tours in October.

BURGER BAR INSIDE A BUS TERMINAL

What history do the walls of an old Greyhound station hold?

In the past, when travelers sought an alternative to driving or flying, Greyhound depots were the go-to transportation hub. Evansville saw the introduction of this speedy mode of transport in 1939. Architect William S. Arrasmith, who designed several Greyhound terminals between 1937 and 1960, was responsible for designing Evansville's. The station's curved corners and blue enameled steel panels echoed the Greyhound buses, a color motif used in other major city terminals that have since been demolished. Despite the decision by the City of Evansville to construct a smaller terminal as a replacement, the iconic structure still stands.

In 2007, Greyhound vacated the station, leaving the building vacant. The City of Evansville then acquired it and donated it to Indiana Landmarks. Indiana Landmarks undertook a restoration project, focusing on the building's exterior panel, steel sash, and glass block windows. The iconic Greyhound dog neon-light sign was restored to its former glory. The restored building was sold to Cunningham Restaurant Group, who utilized the space to establish the BRU Burger Bar Evansville in 2016.

During the restoration process, workers unearthed memorabilia from Greyhound's rich history, including a wallet containing vintage

BRU BURGER BAR EVANSVILLE

WHAT: A restaurant housed in a restored Greyhound terminal

WHERE: 222 Sycamore St., Evansville

COST: Varies (budget-friendly)

PRO TIP: Dogs are welcome in the outdoor dining area, making it a pet-friendly establishment.

The BRU Burger Bar in Evansville is located in a 1939 Greyhound terminal.

photographs and ledger books from 1940 to 1941 that provide a glimpse into the station's daily operations. The best find was a sketchbook filled with illustrations, possibly used to document travels across the country. The restaurant pays homage to the past by incorporating these Greyhound artifacts and memorabilia into its decor. It is a unique place to visit, offering great burgers and history within its walls.

The once-bustling bus stalls were transformed into an outdoor seating area, while the restaurant's kitchen, restrooms, and bar now occupy the former passenger waiting area inside.

THE HOUSE OF DOCTORS

WOLLENMANN HOUSE

WHAT: A historic home turned into a bistro

WHERE: 1150 Main St., Ferdinand

COST: Varies based on menu prices (budget-friendly)

PRO TIP: You can glimpse the home's exterior while driving by or look inside by visiting its current bistro.

Why is this home named after a doctor?

The Wollenmann House, named after Dr. Aloysius "Alois" Wollenmann, has a history of medical professionals residing on its property. Dr. Matthew Kempf, the first doctor to dwell there, became Dr. Wollenmann's father-in-law when the latter doctor married his daughter in 1893. Dr. Wollenmann moved into the house with his wife, establishing Ferdinand's first drugstore (the Adler Apotheke) in an added building in 1897.

In 1903 the Wollenmanns built a distinctive Swiss chalet-style home on the property, with indoor plumbing and European windows, making it the first of its kind in Ferdinand. A dedicated "sick room" within the house served patients and kept the family isolated from illnesses. Dr. Wollenmann, unfortunately, passed away at the age of 48 due to tuberculosis, leaving his son Werner to take over the home. Werner expanded the property by constructing a gift shop next to the house. He and his wife raised a large family of 14 children there, transforming it into the town's hub for gatherings and festivities.

The Wollenmann House continues to serve the community as a bistro and bakery, preserving its legacy for future generations.

However, as time passed, the house's upkeep became overwhelming for Werner's single daughter, who remained in the home until 2010. Recognizing its historical significance, a group of individuals and organizations came together to purchase the house and donate it to the Ferdinand Historical Society. The Wollenmann House found a new purpose in 2013 when it was added to the National Register of Historic Places.

A TIMEPIECE WITH BURIED SECRETS

Could the Colgate Clock be standing above a hidden cemetery?

The Colgate Clock is an iconic timepiece at the site of a former Colgate-Palmolive factory in Clarksville. This colossal clock has a diameter of 40 feet, making it one of the largest clocks in the world. It was built in 1906 and relocated from Jersey City to Clarksville to inaugurate the Colgate-Palmolive plant.

The Colgate-Palmolive plant's history dates back to 1847, when it initially served as Indiana's Reformatory South. Researchers have uncovered numerous records indicating that individuals were likely buried in or near the former plant lot during its time as a state prison and reformatory. These burials may have occurred along the facility's back and side, possibly near railroad tracks. Former Colgate employees have said they saw human remains during excavation work for a new building.

Multiple cemeteries may exist within the area. These burial sites might have been on land sold long ago for infrastructure projects like roads or railways. Alternatively, they could lie beneath the towering Colgate Clock, adding to the site's historical significance and curiosity.

During the devastating 1937 flood, which submerged Clarksville, the clock stood untouched, perched high above the factory. It served as one of the few recognizable markers indicating the location of Clarksville during the flood.

Despite the closing of the Colgate plant in 2008, the iconic clock remains a prominent landmark in the area. Over the decades, the clock's ticking has experienced intermittent pauses, and when it ceases to function, clock enthusiasts immediately notice its absence.

COLGATE-PALMOLIVE CLOCK

WHAT: One of the largest clocks in the world

WHERE: 1410 S Clark Blvd., Clarksville

COST: Free

PRO TIP: The clock is easily viewed from the parking lot in front of the building.

A WILDCAT STORY

What materials were used to create the Aristicat?

To fully understand the Aristicat sculpture, you'll need to know the story of the school it's associated with, Fairview Elementary. Situated near downtown Bloomington, Fairview Elementary is an arts integration school that takes pride in its mascot, the Fairview Wildcat, and incorporating art into the daily classroom learning experience. As part of the Bloomington Entertainment & Arts District (BEAD), the school fosters a unique educational experience taught through the lens of the arts.

The original Fairview School was constructed in 1893, with a 1928 brick addition. After the original building was demolished in 1953, the addition remained operational. "Aristicat, the Fairview Wildcat" was created using salvaged parts from the original school building. The lights from an old entry serve as its eyes, the coal-room door becomes its nose, and a portion of the fire-escape slide forms its mouth. The letters "Fairview," initially displayed on the front of the old building, are now incorporated into the base of the cat. Two mosaic paw prints, created using marble from the windowsills of the old building, are positioned on the ground in front of

Aristicat. These paw prints were the creative work of the sixth graders in 2010.

The Aristicat was designed by students and crafted by local artist Joe LaMantia, whose children were students at Fairview. The wildcat's name, chosen by the sixth-grade class, is a creative blend of "artist" and "cat." Students added their personal touch by painting the Aristicat with their handprints, giving the cat "spots." The words "Fairview Five" are displayed inside the Aristicat's mouth, representing the school's core values: respect, responsibility, safety, personal best, and care.

ARISTICAT SCULPTURE

WHAT: A sculpture created using 1893 school-building parts

WHERE: Fairview Elementary School, 500 7th St., Bloomington

COST: Free

PRO TIP: The sculpture is in the southeast corner of Fairview Elementary's grounds. For the best viewing experience, visit when school is not in session.

"Aristicat" is a large, artsy cat sculpture that stares wide-eyed at the traffic passing. It was created from the school's former 1893 building and designed by the students.

WORLD'S LONGEST TRESTLE BRIDGE

Which railroad bridge holds the title of the world's longest operational train trestle?

The Tulip Trestle, also known as the Tulip Viaduct, Greene County Viaduct, and Bridge X76-6, is a railroad bridge spanning 2,295 feet. It is the longest operational train trestle in the world. Despite its multiple names, the Tulip Trestle is most famous and is considered Greene County's best-kept secret.

Located in Bloomfield, the bridge stretches across Richland Creek, connecting Solsberry and Tulip. Its construction took over a year, and when completed in 1906, it became the longest rail trestle in the United States and the third-longest bridge of its type in the country. The primary purpose of the Tulip Trestle was to transport local coal from Greene County to larger cities such as Chicago.

The Indianapolis Southern Railway constructed the 157-foot-tall bridge with 18 supporting towers. The construction employed primarily Italian immigrant laborers,

TULIP TRESTLE

WHAT: The world's longest operational trestle bridge

WHERE: 3615 N Viaduct Rd., Bloomfield

COST: Free

PRO TIP: Pack a picnic or grab a bite from a local restaurant like the Yoho General Store to enjoy at the Tulip Trestle Observation Deck.

While the train lacks a public schedule and its arrival time varies daily, locals suggest the best time to catch a glimpse of a train is typically between 4 and 6 p.m.

who received a substantial wage of 30 cents per hour in 1906. Passenger trains crossed the viaduct initially, but this practice ended in 1948. Crossing the bridge would have been daunting for individuals with a fear of heights.

Throughout the day, trains operated by the Indiana Rail Road Company cross the Tulip Trestle, transporting coal. Visitors can witness these trains in motion from the Tulip Trestle Observation Deck. The deck offers a parking area, picnic tables, informative signs, a "Free Little Library," paved "track plank" path, and a portable toilet for visitors' convenience. The observation deck is ideal for capturing photographs and enjoying panoramic views.

A PIECE OF HEAVEN ALONG THE OHIO RIVER

GOD'S GARDEN

WHAT: A peaceful prayer garden along the Ohio River

WHERE: 119 W Jennings St., Newburgh

COST: Free

PRO TIP: While parking in front of the garden is restricted to one or two vehicles, downtown Newburgh also offers parking options within convenient walking distance.

Where in Newburgh can you find a hidden sanctuary?

I often seek solace in hidden gems where I can rest, meditate, and savor a good book. Frequently overlooked and underappreciated, these places offer a serene atmosphere that fosters a connection with nature and inner peace. I knew I had to visit when I first heard about "God's Garden" in Newburgh. This sanctuary has no dedicated website or social media page but exists through word-of-mouth and local recommendations.

In the backyard of Mary Ann and Jim Wilsbacher's private property lies a small garden, open to the public. As you enter, a sign greets you, "Welcome to God's Garden . . . Come in any time, walk around, relax in the gazebo, and soak in God's peace and beauty." A brick sidewalk leads you to the gazebo, offering comfortable chairs to enjoy the view of the garden and the Ohio River beyond. Flowers, lawn ornaments, and fountains adorn the vibrant greenscape and manicured lawn. Statues, plaques, and verses are scattered throughout the garden as gentle reminders of hope and peace.

During your visit on a weekend or during the spring, you might encounter a wedding ceremony or photographers capturing moments of a prom. However, when I visited, I had the opportunity to be the sole visitor in the garden. This allowed me to sit and reflect peacefully, with the entire garden to myself.

God's Garden is located along the Newburgh Riverwalk and overlooks the Ohio River. The owners have opened this hidden gem for the public to enjoy.

A GROTTO BUILT FROM GEODES

Where is the grotto built on a former handball court?

Father Phillip Ottavi spent over a decade constructing the Geode Grotto in Jasper. An Italian immigrant, Father Ottavi had lost his parents in the devastating Messina earthquake of 1908. The tragedy left him orphaned and filled with anger toward the rock and rubble that had taken his family. Father Ottavi turned to his faith to overcome his anger and became a priest. Inspired by the beautiful Catholic grottos he had seen in Europe, he created a grotto out of the material that had caused him so much pain. The Geode Grotto was the result of his efforts.

In southern Indiana, where geodes are plentiful, the Providence Home grotto was constructed between 1960 and 1970 under the guidance of Father Ottavi. The grotto, which covers four city blocks, was built on a former handball-court site and replicates the famous grotto at Lourdes in France. Geodes, soft rocks filled with crystal centers,

GEODE GROTTO

WHAT: A grotto made from Indiana geodes

WHERE: 520 W 9th St., Jasper

COST: Free

PRO TIP: Behind the Cathedral Health Care Center is a parking lot; street parking is also an option.

Peace and solace lie at the heart of the grotto's origins. In the 1950s, a priest struggling to accept his tragedy constructed the shrine.

were primarily sourced from nearby Heltonville. Residents and volunteers worked together to create this remarkable structure.

The Geode Grotto showcases two main shrines, seven smaller ones, white Carrara marble statues imported from Italy, fountains, planters, a spacious 12-foot cave-like opening, and picturesque gardens. Each planter weighs an impressive 2,500 pounds, adding to the grandeur of this unique attraction.

A HARDWARE STORE TIME CAPSULE

Which hardware store is a National Historic Landmark?

Established almost 130 years ago, the L. H. Sturm Hardware Co. store has been a family-run business for four generations. Step inside and it's like stepping back in time into a living-history museum. The top shelves of the store are adorned with antiques such as a butter churn, old fans, and a tricycle. As you move higher up the shelves, the eras represented become older, with more modern hardware and housewares displayed on the floor level. Among the notable features of the store is a giant Florence Hot Air Blast coal stove, a relic from 1923. An old-fashioned rolling wooden ladder reaches hard-to-reach items, adding to the store's charm.

Constructed in 1886 and acquired by the Sturm family in 1895, the hardware store is one of Indiana's oldest continuously family-operated hardware stores. In 2004, it was recognized as a historical landmark by being listed on the National Register of Historic Places.

The L. H. Sturm Hardware Co. sells everything from wine and beer-making supplies to cast iron cookware, knives, and hard-to-find replacement parts.

The storefront, creaky floors, and ceilings all feature original woodwork, showcasing the store's age.

Standing tall across the street from the courthouse, the three-story building is accessible through a winding staircase or freight elevator. The second floor once served as a dentist's office, while the third floor accommodated the Knights of Pythias.

L. H. STURM HARDWARE CO.

WHAT: The oldest continuously family-operated hardware store in the state

WHERE: 516 Main St., Jasper

COST: Free

PRO TIP: Include a visit to the Jasper Geode Grotto on your itinerary while you're in Jasper.

THE ONLY OPERATIONAL ROTARY JAIL IN THE COUNTRY

Is this jail haunted by the ghost of murderer John Coffee?

In 1881, the first of 18 rotary jails was constructed in Crawfordsville. This jail is the only operational structure of the three remaining rotary jails in the country. The design prioritized the safety of prisoners and the security of jailers. The rotary design was considered a mechanical masterpiece, and the jail provided inmates with remarkable amenities, including three hot meals daily, regular bathing, clean clothing, and access to medical care. Each cell featured a toilet, an uncommon luxury for most homes in Crawfordsville at that time.

The jail is connected to what is now a museum and was once the sheriff's residence. The 32-ton, two-story circular structure sits on 16 roller bearings and can be rotated with a hand crank. Museum guides rotate the crank to showcase the rotary jail's rotation, which appears challenging. Each floor has one doorway that provides access to each cell only when the hand crank aligns the cell with the doorway.

According to inspection reports, the Crawfordsville jail was deemed unsafe as early as 1913 despite its original purpose of serving human concerns. In 1973, a new prison was constructed, leading to the closure of the rotary jail. A few

---

In 1975, the Rotary Jail, along with the former sheriff's residence, was included in the National Register of Historic Places as part of a museum dedicated to preserving and showcasing Montgomery County's history.

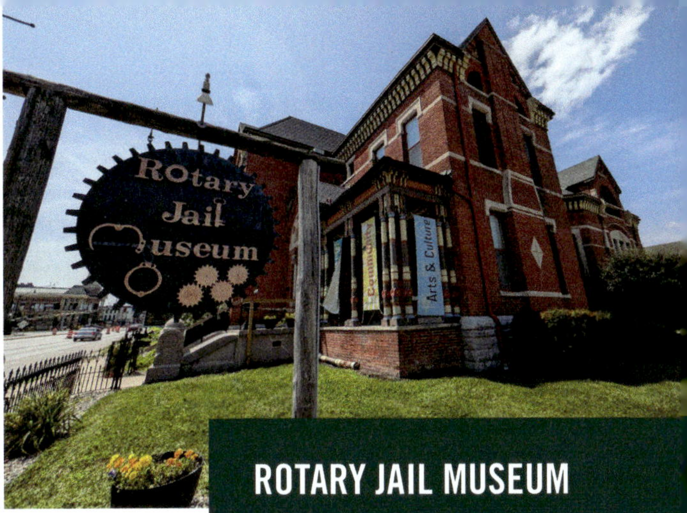

ROTARY JAIL MUSEUM

WHAT: Museum and operating rotary jail

WHERE: 225 N Washington St., Crawfordsville

COST: Fee for admission

PRO TIP: The museum doesn't have a dedicated parking lot; however, visitors can access free street parking in front and surrounding the museum.

Bottom: *In 1918, during confinement in this high-security cell, an inmate ignited the mattress using a hidden match, resulting in a fire. Tragically, smoke inhalation claimed the inmate's life.*

years later, the jail became a museum. Visitors to the museum can walk through the home and jail, collectively resembling a 19th-century middle-class home from the outside.

In 1885, the notorious murder case involving John Coffee landed Coffee in the Crawfordsville Rotary Jail. After being arrested, Coffee was convicted of several murders and sentenced to death by hanging. The execution, held on the jail grounds, encountered multiple obstacles when the rope snapped twice, requiring three attempts to carry out the sentence. Coffee's execution was one of two to occur at this location, and rumors persist that the jail remains haunted by his presence.

THE *BEN-HUR* STUDY

GENERAL LEW WALLACE STUDY & MUSEUM

WHAT: The study and museum of *Ben-Hur*'s author

WHERE: 200 Wallace Ave., Crawfordsville

COST: Fee for admission; free to walk the grounds

PRO TIP: Tours are by appointment only and can be made online.

Which famous author built his study in Crawfordsville?

Tucked away in a charming Crawfordsville neighborhood is the study of General Lew Wallace, author of the acclaimed religious novel *Ben-Hur: A Tale of the Christ* (1880). Wallace, a multi-faceted individual, was also a major general in the Union Army, a military judge, and an ambassador to the Ottoman Empire. His talents extended beyond literature, encompassing painting and invention as well. *Ben-Hur* became the best-selling novel of the 19th century and was later adapted into a film in 1959 starring actor Charlton Heston.

Between 1895 and 1898, Wallace, who resided in Crawfordsville, constructed his study on the same plot as his residence. The study stands as an architectural masterpiece, boasting an impressive three-story tower. It features a basement equipped with a kitchen, bathroom, and wine cellar. The property spans over three acres of sprawling greenspace, landscaped gardens, and a reflecting pool

(subsequently filled in). The limestone and brick study initially showcased a moat encircling it, which Wallace later filled in for safety reasons.

On the outside of the study, each side of the building features four distinct representations from his novels *Ben-Hur* and *Why Constantinople Fell*. Upon entering, visitors are greeted by the main room, which has a stunning stained-glass skylight window that dominates the ceiling. The room includes bookcases filled with Wallace's personal collection, a nook, a gas fireplace, and various memorabilia displays—including the original *Ben-Hur* film armor.

Visitors can tour the study, starting with an introductory film in the Carriage House.

The General Lew Wallace Study is a National Historic Landmark recipient of the National Medal from the Federal Institute of Museum and Library Services.

A TV STAR'S NONPROFIT ARCADE

What do Rupert from the show *Survivor* and an arcade have in common?

Shelbyville's own Rupert Boneham made his reality television debut in 2003 as a contestant on the hit show *Survivor*. He competed on the show four times and became the first contestant to complete consecutive seasons. Rupert's popularity with viewers earned him the title of "fan favorite," and he was awarded $1 million from the show. A significant portion of his winnings established Rupert's Kids, a nonprofit organization.

RUPERT'S KIDS ARCADE

WHAT: Nonprofit classic video arcade

WHERE: 109 S Harrison St., Shelbyville

COST: Fee for unlimited play

PRO TIP: Check out Rupert's Kids Arcade for special events and hours.

Rupert's Kids is an organization dedicated to empowering at-risk youth and guiding them toward a positive path. Born from Rupert's experiences as a struggling teen, this nonprofit aims to uplift those in his community who face similar challenges. Through its programs and resources, Rupert's Kids provides a lifeline to at-risk youth, helping them regain their footing and build a brighter future.

Are you curious about the connection between Rupert, his organization, and an arcade? Rupert established Rupert's Kids Arcade, a classic arcade where all proceeds are donated

With some luck, you might run into Rupert, who occasionally graces the arcade and parties with his presence.

to his charity. The arcade offers diverse entertainment options in downtown Shelbyville, including video games, pinball machines, and skee-ball. Visitors can choose between one-hour or all-day unlimited play. The arcade is available for rent, providing a unique venue for parties and events.

You can visit the arcade for pinball nostalgia with beloved classics like Whirlwind, Jaws, Jurassic Park, and Foo Fighters—or experience video game bowling with Silver Strike Bowling and a hunting adventure with Big Buck Hunter. Relive the golden era of gaming with Donkey Kong, Pac-Man, or Burger Time. For a retro gaming adventure, the challenge of Comix Zone on the Sega Genesis or quests with Metroid and the Legend of Zelda on the Nintendo are available. These are just a few of the gaming experiences at the arcade.

AN ITALIAN POW CHAPEL

Why is there a POW chapel in the woods?

In 1943, during World War II, Camp Atterbury in Franklin, Indiana, housed 3,000 Italian prisoners of war (POWs). Unlike many other POW camps, Camp Atterbury gave its prisoners respect and care, including unlimited meals, beds with mattresses, recreational activities, and religious freedom. Historians have documented that these POWs regarded their time in American custody as preferable to their harrowing experiences as soldiers in Europe, finding solace at Camp Atterbury.

Under the guidance and encouragement of a US Army chaplain, who conducted Sunday Masses at the camp, the POWs transformed leftover bricks and stucco into an Italian chapel on the property. Known as the "Chapel in the Meadow," its walls were painted using flowers and berries. Talented

CAMP ATTERBURY POW CHAPEL

WHAT: A restored 1943 chapel built by Italian POWs

WHERE: 2949 E North St., Franklin

COST: Free

PRO TIP: Watch for the signs; the chapel is a few miles from the Camp Atterbury base.

Italian artists among the POWs depicted scenes of war and their living conditions through murals that featured American soldiers, cherubs, and religious figures like Jesus and the Virgin Mary. The chapel's altar was painted to resemble marble, while the walls were given a Mediterranean blue hue.

After the war, the prisoners aligned with the Allies or returned to their homes—the chapel was abandoned for several decades. In the 1990s, with the assistance of the Indiana Italian Heritage Society, the chapel and its paintings underwent restoration. Today, visitors, including descendants of the Italian POWs, can visit the 11 by 16-foot chapel located within Camp Atterbury. Nestled discreetly within a wooded area near Stone Arch Lake, the chapel is the sole remaining structure out of approximately 100 buildings that once made up the POW camp, situated a few miles from the base.

The Camp Atterbury Museum is also in the Camp Atterbury Welcome Center. It's free and open to the public.

A JAPANESE OASIS

Why are there Japanese lanterns and giant koi fish in this alley?

Japanese culture flourishes within Kuji Alley, a tribute to Franklin, Indiana's sister city, Kuji, Japan. Over the years, hundreds of students, professionals, club members, and city officials have exchanged visits between the two cities. This unique sister-city relationship is attributed to the efforts of Thomasine "Tommy" Allen, a 1911 graduate of Franklin College. Driven by her faith, Allen was a Baptist missionary in Japan from 1915 to 1976. Her dedication led her to become a resident of Kuji, where her final resting place is on a hill overlooking the city near the church she founded, a testament to her impact on the community.

Inspired by the coastal town of Kuji, where fishing is a primary source of income, artist Greg Potter set out to capture the region's essence with the alley's murals. Potter created a koi-fish mural covering the walls and the ground. The lifelike mural gives the illusion of oversized koi fish swimming beneath and around the viewer, creating an immersive experience.

In the alley, a display of 70 Japanese lanterns, adorned with the word "Kuji" in Japanese characters, gently sway overhead, paying homage to Franklin's sister city. On the north wall, a metal cherry blossom tree adorned with 800 metal cherry blossoms forms a wave-like pattern, complemented by an additional 600 metal cherry blossoms. Beneath this blossoming wall is a small Japanese footbridge.

Originating in 1961, the remarkable Kuji-Franklin bond is Indiana's longest sister-city relationship.

Just a few blocks away, Artcraft Alley is another art installation in Franklin. Two hundred multi-colored stars are strung above the alleyway, and blacklights in the alley help the stars to glow at night.

KUJI ALLEY

WHAT: Japanese art installation in an alley

WHERE: 39 E Court St., Franklin

COST: Free

PRO TIP: Located in the alley, across from the courthouse.

A GARDEN OF VINTAGE GAS STATION SIGNS

What "sign"-ificance does a collection of vintage service station signs have in Whiteland?

Collector Alan Ray Whitaker, also known as the "sign guy," has assembled an impressive collection of over 50 oval gas-station signs in his yard. Since 2016, he has gathered vintage signs from brands like Gulf, Lion, Sinclair, 76, and Texaco. These free-standing signs, ranging in age from 1934 to 1961, stand tall on 18-foot poles, forming a distinctive U-shape in a side yard adjacent to Whitaker's shop.

The Garden of Gas Station Signs is more than just a collection of signs; it is a labor of love. Whitaker's passion for preserving and sharing this piece of automotive history is evident in every inch of the sign garden.

Amidst the retro sign garden, a vintage glowing Roto-Sphere

GARDEN OF GAS STATION SIGNS

WHAT: A garden with 36 free-standing gas station signs

WHERE: 649 Brewer St., Whiteland

COST: Free

PRO TIP: The sign garden is located just off Interstate 65, making it a terrific road trip stop.

takes center stage. This 1964 space-age rotating neon sign, restored by Whitaker, once graced the now-closed Catalina Motel in Lexington, Kentucky. During their heyday in the 1960s, Roto-Spheres were popular for businesses like the Catalina Motel. This particular Roto-Sphere, designated as #160, is a creation of Warren Milks, who designed and built it.

While situated on private property, this hidden gem is accessible for viewing. It offers a glimpse into a bygone era when gas stations were adorned with vibrant and eye-catching signs. The indoor shop, known as the "Toy Box," is closed to the public unless you're lucky enough to get a private tour by Whitaker himself.

Some visitors have gotten a chance to see the inside of Whitaker's shop, the "Toy Box," featuring indoor collector items like gas-pump globes, pinball machines, neon clocks, and more gas station signs.

THE HOME WHERE LITTLE ORPHAN ANNIE LIVED

Was Little Orphan Annie a real person?

Growing up in Greenfield during the 1850s and 1860s, Indiana poet James Whitcomb Riley found inspiration for his 1,000 works of dialect and children's poems, including the source material for "Little Orphant Annie," a poem he penned in 1885 (later misprinted as "Little Orphan Annie"). Riley's childhood home on Main Street was a muse for many of his literary creations. "Little Orphan Annie" captivated audiences through various mediums, including an American comic strip in 1924, a radio show in 1930, and a famous Broadway musical in 1977.

It may surprise you to learn that a real person inspired the character of Little Orphant Annie in James Whitcomb Riley's poem. During the Civil War, Riley's mother, Elizabeth, hired a 12-year-old orphan named Mary Alice "Allie" Smith to help with household chores. Riley drew inspiration from Mary Alice when writing "Little Orphant Annie."

Mary Alice, the real "Annie," was a country girl from Liberty, Indiana, born in 1850, just a year older than Riley. In exchange for her assistance, she resided with the Riley family. Mary Alice

---

Interestingly, the poem was initially titled "Little Orphan Allie" but was mistakenly published as "Little Orphant Annie" due to a printer's error, which Riley decided to keep.

RILEY BIRTHPLACE AND MUSEUM

WHAT: The boyhood home of James Whitcomb Riley

WHERE: 250 W Main St., Greenfield

COST: Fee for admission

PRO TIP: Don't be confused with the Riley Museum Home, located in Indianapolis, where Riley lived during the last decades of his life.

developed a close friendship with the children, captivating them with fascinating and spooky stories. The stairway in the Riley home particularly captivated her. She referred to it as the "stairway to heaven" and gave each step a name.

The Riley Boyhood Home offers visitors a glimpse of the Greenfield home referenced in Riley's poems. At the top of the staircase, visitors can see where Mary Alice slept during her stay there. Her small section was located near the boys' bedroom. Additionally, the museum boasts a 1965 Little Orphan Annie doll by Madame Alexander and other artifacts.

A RAILROAD TREASURE TROVE

What surprises can I find in rural Monon?

Away from the hustle and bustle of Indianapolis and Lafayette sits a treasure trove for railroad enthusiasts: Monon Connection Museum. Although it may be off the beaten path, the museum's location adds charm. Outside, the lawn is adorned with cabooses and cranes, instantly capturing one's attention. Inside is a world of railroad history, with over 6,500 artifacts on display. Guided tours are available, and for those who want to extend their train-themed experience, the attached Whistle Stop Restaurant offers a dining option. Whether you're a serious train enthusiast or just looking for a unique adventure, the Monon Connection Museum is a hidden Indiana destination.

The museum offers guided tours every hour. Visitors can take a self-guided tour or participate in the guided tours, which take them through four rooms filled with various displays. From cabooses and railcars to Tiffany windows, there's something for everyone to enjoy. The museum's highlight is the Flager Car, which boasts hand-carved woodwork from the Canary Islands, a marble fireplace, and a chandelier.

MONON CONNECTION MUSEUM

WHAT: Indiana's largest privately owned railroad museum

WHERE: 10012 US-421, Monon

COST: Fee for admission

PRO TIP: Patrons can enjoy home-cooked meals at the museum's restaurant, Whistle Stop, while an operating G-scale model train whizzes overhead.

Other attractions include a model-train layout, a train depot, and a collectibles collection.

Take advantage of the opportunity to capture a memorable photo outside the entrance, where a vintage red British telephone booth with the original phone awaits.

The Caboose Park in Monon offers a unique photo opportunity with the historic red caboose of the Monon Railroad and its accompanying historical marker.

A WORLD RECORD-HOLDING BALL

What is a 10,000-pound ball of paint?

In Alexandria, a surprising world record can be found—the largest ball of paint. One might wonder how a ball of paint came to be and how it earned its record status. Visiting Michael and Glenda Carmichael's barn will provide the answers.

In 1997, a weird tradition was born when Michael and his son dipped a baseball in blue house paint. Over the years, they added layer after layer of paint until the ball became a world-record holder. As of the book's writing, this baseball weighed over 10,000 pounds and had almost 30,000 layers of paint. Its extraordinary size required its own dwelling, a barn fortified with beams, allowing the ball to hang and visitors to become world-record holders.

Visitors are invited to call and schedule an appointment to paint a

WORLD'S LARGEST BALL OF PAINT

WHAT: The world's largest ball of paint

WHERE: 10696 N 200 W, Alexandria

COST: Free

PRO TIP: Wear clothes you don't mind potentially getting paint on.

layer on the ball, officially becoming the record-holder for the World's Largest Ball of Paint until another visitor arrives. During my visit, I chose blue, the most popular color option, and painted layer 27,814. Visitors can select their preferred paint color, sign the guest book (or wall or ceiling), and receive a certificate. People from over 50 countries, including the Oak Ridge Boys, who sang "Elvira" while painting their layer, have visited.

Appointments must be made in advance. Call the Carmichaels at 765-724-4008.

ONE SCHOOL IN TWO STATES

Why is the school gymnasium divided into two distinct state parts?

COLLEGE CORNER UNION ELEMENTARY

WHAT: The only joint-state school district in Indiana

WHERE: Indiana St., West College Corner

COST: Free

PRO TIP: Because the school has multiple addresses, be sure GPS directs you correctly.

During its 111-year history, the Union School served as two distinct schools within the same building, each with its own administration, funding, and entry. The Indiana side was the Union Township School, while the Ohio side was College Corner Union School. The state border served as a physical divide between them, with a line still visible on the flagpole, entrances, and gymnasium's center, marking the territorial separation.

In 1995, the school district transitioned to operate under Indiana law. During this transition, Ohio students were "transferred" to the school, allowing the State of Ohio to reimburse the State of Indiana for their education. This led to a name change for the school, now known as the Union County-College Corner Joint State School District (UC/CC). This change is noteworthy because UC/CC is the last remaining joint state school district between Ohio and Indiana and potentially the only one of its kind left in the United States.

For an ideal glimpse of this unique school, plan your trip during breaks when school is not in session, such as summer vacation, evenings, weekends, or holidays.

Constructed in 1893, the original schoolhouse was enlarged by an addition built in 1926. The addition features a central stone marker on the state line and includes two arched doorways, one representing Indiana and the other representing Ohio. The original 1893 Union School bell is prominently displayed at the front entrance on the south side, positioned between the Indiana and Ohio entrances. An Ohio Historic Marker can be found behind the schoolhouse on the north side, between the Indiana and Ohio entrances.

THE COUPLE BURIED IN A STATE PARK

Who is buried on Trail 11?

An often overlooked but captivating trail holds hidden treasures in Indiana's Turkey Run State Park, celebrated for its rugged trails and stunning canyons. Trail 11 is relatively easy and seemingly uninteresting but leads to historic sites and secrets that will surprise visitors. Constructed in 1871 and rebuilt in 1923, the Log Church is a testament to the region's religious legacy. It was once the park's administrative building. In 2001, the church earned a spot on the National Register of Historic Places. During the summer, nondenominational services are held every Sunday at 10 a.m.

Richard Lieber's foresight enabled Indiana to become one of the first states to establish a system of state parks, preserving significant natural areas. He and author Juliet Strauss, the founder of the Woman's Press Club of Indiana, worked tirelessly to raise funds and negotiate the land purchase for Turkey Run in 1916.

Trail 11 is a short 0.5-mile hike above Turkey Run Hollow. Among the more renowned spots on this trail are the Log Church and the Lieber Memorial.

Lieber passed away in 1944, and his ashes, along with those of his wife, Emma, now rest at the base of the Colonel Richard Lieber memorial within the park. In my eyes, their story represents a love story forged through a shared love of conservation and nature. Richard Lieber, accompanied by his wife, passed away at McCormick Creek State Park. They had been visiting the park together, hoping to rest and aid Emma's recovery from an illness, when Lieber suffered a heart attack.

In recognition of Strauss's contributions, the Woman's Press Club of Indiana erected a memorial to her in 1922. The sculpture, titled *Subjugation*, captures the essence of Strauss's writings and can be found near the entrance of Trail 11.

TURKEY RUN STATE PARK, TRAIL 11

WHAT: Resting place of Indiana's state park founder

WHERE: 8121 E Park Rd., Marshall

COST: Fee for admission

PRO TIP: Church services are held in the historic Log Church on Sundays between Good Friday and Labor Day.

OUTLAWS AND ARTIFACTS

HAMILTON COUNTY MUSEUM OF HISTORY AND OLD SHERIFF'S RESIDENCE AND JAIL

WHAT: Historic jail that housed famous inmates

WHERE: 810 Conner St., Noblesville

COST: Donation-based admission

PRO TIP: During weekdays, there is free two-hour street parking around the Square. For longer durations, free parking is available at the Levinson parking garage.

What is the connection between Charles Manson and Noblesville?

In Noblesville's downtown square is the historic Hamilton County Sheriff's Residence and Jail, dating back to 1876. Now transformed into the Museum of History, this site welcomes visitors to explore its rich past. Among its notable inmates were Charles Manson, who spent time within its walls at the age of 15 for theft, and D. C. Stephenson, a Ku Klux Klan leader. Manson, a runaway, was held in the jail until his transfer back to the Plainfield Boys School.

The jail remained operational until 1977, when a new jail was constructed. Since then, the building has been unoccupied. The first floor contained four cells exclusively for men, while the second floor housed juvenile cells that were occasionally used to accommodate adult overflow. The third floor features Victorian cells designed for female inmates or individuals requiring isolation from the general jail population, such as Stephenson. It is the most original part of the building, as the walls have been left unpainted to preserve the graffiti.

The sheriff's home includes a parlor with a Kimball pump organ and fireplace, foyers leading to bedrooms via a grand staircase, and a Victorian-era bedroom containing antiques such as a spinning wheel and sewing machines. The kitchen served both the family and the jail. A small staff and the family prepared meals for the inmates. The sheriff's wife also served as the matron for female and child prisoners.

The Hamilton County Sheriff's Residence and Jail, which are part of the museum, contain exhibits related to the county's history, including genealogy records and old photographs.

NEW YORK CITY'S FIRST SKYSCRAPER IN A PARK

How did NYC's first skyscraper find a home in Holliday Park?

In the 1950s, the owners of the St. Paul Building, New York's first skyscraper, removed massive statues crafted from Indiana limestone from the building's summit. These statues, collectively known as *The Races of Man*, were valued at $150,000 and weighed eight tons each.

The statues found a new home in Holliday Park, Indianapolis, where Elmer Taflinger was hired to incorporate them into a landscape design. Taflinger's vision included reflecting ponds, foundations, and remnants of demolished buildings from the city, creating the Ruins, which took over two decades to complete. As a finishing touch, Taflinger added six columns encircling the reflection pool, resulting in an outdoor art installation providing visitors with space to enjoy.

In the summer, Holliday Park regularly hosts "Rock the Ruins" outdoor concerts. Additionally, there are hiking trails, a playground, a nature center, and access to the White River.

The Ruins, dedicated in 1973, represent the American Republic, symbolizing the unity of men and women of all races working toward freedom and justice. Taflinger expanded the design, adding a vast landscape and a reflecting pool to create Constitution Mall.

The design incorporates elements from Indianapolis's past. These include a horse trough that once resided at the base of a notable monument in Fountain Square, Greek columns salvaged from the Sister of the Good Shepherd Convent, and sculptures of Greek goddesses that adorned the façade of Marion County Courthouse—all remnants of the city's history.

In 2016, the Friends of Holliday Park revitalized the Ruins, updating it with a children's water table, shimmer fountain, benches, trees, and new gardens. To enhance the visitor experience, outdoor restrooms were also added and are available from April through October.

HOLLIDAY PARK

WHAT: A park preserving parts of former Indianapolis buildings and even a New York one

WHERE: 6363 Spring Mill Rd., Indianapolis

COST: Free

PRO TIP: If visiting during the summer, check their events calendar beforehand.

COFFEE IN A FORMER MENTAL HOSPITAL

What's brewing in this former psychiatric hospital?

In a rare opportunity, visitors can explore the historic grounds of a former mental hospital, which now houses an unexpected treasure: a delightful craft-coffee shop. Mansion Society, owned by mother-daughter duo Zoraida and Ana Lezama, is on the grounds of the former Central State Mansion. Once a mental hospital, the building was repurposed into apartments, and this hidden gem is tucked away in the lobby.

The psychiatric hospital operated for over 150 years and is an infamous part of Indianapolis's history. This history lends Mansion Society a curious charm that entices coffee enthusiasts and those intrigued by a spooky ambiance. Despite rumors of paranormal activity and ghosts haunting the premises, the lobby has been transformed into a cozy, vintage café that exudes beauty and allure. A vintage bar and cafeteria-style stools and seating add to the café's unique character.

Traces of the hospital's past are still visible, with many

MANSION SOCIETY

WHAT: A coffee shop in a former mental hospital

WHERE: 202 Steeples Blvd., Indianapolis

COST: Free to visit; varies based on menu prices (budget-friendly)

PRO TIP: While visiting the coffee shop, you can also schedule a tour of the Indiana Medical History Museum in the former Pathology Building on the same grounds.

original doors, fixtures, and ceramic tiles preserved within the building's structure. The Lezamas have embraced this vintage theme and curated a coffee shop showcasing items dating back to the 1940s, sourced from thrift stores and estate sales. Stepping into Mansion Society feels like a journey through time, where beverages are served in mugs and glasses placed on silver plates, and patrons relax with views of the pool and landscaped grounds at the rear of the building.

The Mansion Society is a minority, women-owned coffee shop that makes its own syrups, concentrates, and sauces in-house.

THE BUILDING WITH BRAINS

What is the secret behind the jars of brains?

Within the Old Pathology Building of the Indiana Medical History Museum, an intriguing exhibit presents itself: jars containing preserved human brains. The museum, situated on the grounds of the former Central State Hospital, was known as the "Indiana Hospital for the Insane" when it opened in 1848. Located near Indianapolis's west side, this building is the oldest surviving pathology facility in the country and is on the National Register of Historic Places.

In 1896, the hospital established the Medical College of Indiana and Pathological Department to provide research and treatment for patients suffering from mental disorders, alcoholism, dementia, and epilepsy at the hospital. Operational until the 1960s, the department was later transformed into a museum in 1969, preserving its scientifically equipped interior and specimens. Ultimately, the hospital's doors closed in 1994 following scandals of patient abuse.

The college is also tied to the infamous murder of Dr. Helene Knabe. Dr. Knabe graduated from the Medical College of Indiana in 1904 and began her career only to be found murdered in 1911—a murder that remains unsolved.

Visitors to the museum can sit in the teaching amphitheater, where Dr. Knabe was the only student selected by the director of pathology to teach courses to underclassmen. Exhibits are viewable in the laboratories once dedicated to bacteriology,

---

The Indiana Medical History Museum is a testament to the groundbreaking efforts and discoveries that have shaped our understanding of mental health and its treatment.

In the chemistry laboratory, visitors can observe original plumbing fixtures alongside a hand-cranked, two-vial centrifuge and original bottles.

clinical chemistry, histology, and photography. Additionally, there is a library, a reception room, and a records room. The autopsy room and anatomical museum exhibit preserved specimens, primarily brains, and aren't for those who get queasy. Among the museums I've encountered, it stands out as one of the most intriguing, catering to curious minds.

INDIANA MEDICAL HISTORY MUSEUM

WHAT: History museum located on former insane-asylum grounds

WHERE: 3270 Kirkbride Way, Indianapolis

COST: Fee for admission

PRO TIP: Public museum tours are by appointment only and can be made online. Tours aren't suggested for younger children, as the topics may be disturbing.

A ROCK-AND-ROLL TIME CAPSULE

Did the King really leave the building?

On June 26, 1977, inside the Indianapolis Market Square Arena, Elvis Presley performed his final concert. Once a popular venue, the arena welcomed 18,000 enthusiastic fans eager to witness Elvis's electrifying performance. The concert, scheduled for 8:30 p.m., faced a delay due to Elvis's tardiness, and he eventually graced the stage at 10 p.m. During the concert, Elvis enthralled the audience with his signature tunes, including "Jailhouse Rock," "Don't Be Cruel," and "Can't Help Falling in Love." Tragically, Elvis's life ended six weeks after this concert, making it his last performance.

ELVIS'S FINAL CONCERT PLAQUE

WHAT: A historic plaque commemorating Elvis's final concert

WHERE: 320 E Market St., Indianapolis

COST: Free

PRO TIP: The memorial is on the corner of Alabama and Market Streets, in front of Whole Foods Market, along the Indianapolis Cultural Trail.

The Market Square Arena, once a prominent landmark, no longer exists. In its place is a plaque memorializing Elvis's last concert. It was dedicated in 2002, paying homage to the former arena's significance. In 2018, a formal ceremony was held to rededicate the plaque and honor the memory of Elvis Presley. At the ceremony, peanut butter and banana crepes were served as a tribute to Presley's love for peanut butter and banana sandwiches.

A surprise lies hidden within the plaque—a time capsule encased within its structure. Inside the capsule are pieces of history: a scarf tossed by Elvis to a fan during his final concert,

Encased in the plaque is an original June 26, 1977, ticket stub for Elvis in concert at Market Square Arena.

a cassette recording capturing the performance, tour photographs, a Graceland promotional catalog, and a heartwarming collection of hundreds of handwritten notes penned by fans. This time capsule holds a wealth of memories and is carefully preserved to be unveiled on June 26, 2102, a century after the plaque's re-dedication.

The Elvis Final Concert Plaque showcases an original ticket from the concert and a map of Market Square Arena.

A CYCLING STADIUM

MAJOR TAYLOR VELODROME AT INDY CYCLOPEX

WHAT: One of the few active velodromes in the US

WHERE: 3649 Cold Spring Rd., Indianapolis

COST: Free for spectators, fee for admission to cycle

PRO TIP: The velodrome season is April through September and includes programming for all levels of cyclists, including a regular schedule of coached and open-track riding sessions.

Why is there a stadium cycle-racing track in Indianapolis?

Nineteenth-century Indianapolis cycling icon Marshall Walter "Major" Taylor made history by becoming the first African American athlete to join an integrated professional team and the first black cyclist to hold a world record in 1898. A renowned champion, Taylor had racing skills and showcased his talents in and around Indianapolis. In 1932, he retired from professional racing, leaving an impactful legacy. As a tribute to his achievements, the Major Taylor Velodrome was constructed in 1982 in his honor, recognizing his contributions to the cycling world.

If you aren't familiar with cycling, you might wonder what a velodrome is. I was. It is a stadium cycle-racing track that, in my opinion, resembles a smaller version of the iconic Indy 500 track but for cycling. For those curious about the specifics, the track measures 333.34 meters in length and features steep 28-degree banked turns and 9-degree straights.

The Major Taylor Velodrome is an engineering marvel built into the side of a knoll and atop a natural flood plain. It is a part of the Indy Cycloplex, a cycling-dedicated public park overseen by Marian University. This velodrome, a national-caliber BMX track, and a cyclocross course are the three state-of-the-art venues at the Indy Cycloplex. The velodrome hosts regional and national competitions, training sessions, clinics, and open ride sessions, fostering a vibrant cycling community each year.

Indianapolis is home to the Major Taylor Velodrome, one of the few active velodromes in the United States.

THE TUBERCULOSIS HOSPITAL

Is this site haunted or just a thrilling place to explore?

From 1908 to 1968, the Indiana State Sanatorium served as Indiana's primary tuberculosis hospital. Following that, it was repurposed as a nursing home and a private mental healthcare facility. Today, the expansive 200-acre complex still encompasses the buildings, now abandoned, and supporting structures, including an extensive network of steam tunnels. The site also featured a greenhouse, a dairy barn, and a power plant.

In 1976, the complex was revived as the Lee Alan Bryant Health Care Center, operating as a nursing home and private mental hospital until 2011. However, many items, including hospital beds and equipment, were left behind when it closed, creating an eerie time capsule of the hospital's past. The sheer volume of abandoned items, including clothing, photographs, and medical supplies, is astonishing.

Following the hospital's closure, patients were relocated, leaving the site vacant and vulnerable to vandalism and trespassing. In 2020, the complex was sold, marking the beginning of the Sanatorium Project, an ambitious endeavor to restore the dilapidated site. However, the sheer scale of the buildings means that this undertaking will be lengthy.

Since its exploration, the Indiana State Sanatorium has attracted numerous investigators and documentary film teams, including the *Destination Fear* team.

A network of tunnels linked the pavilion, administrative building, and powerhouse, serving as conduits for essential services such as pipes, electrical wiring, and heating systems.

INDIANA STATE SANATORIUM

WHAT: Historic tuberculosis hospital

WHERE: 3838 E Old 36 Rd., Rockville

COST: Fee for admission

PRO TIP: Please be respectful of Indiana State Sanatorium's private property and book your reservations before going or when the gates are open. Wear comfortable shoes; there is quite a bit of walking!

The site now offers guided tours for paranormal investigations, photography, and urban exploration. Visitors with tickets can access the 1908 hospital tunnels, the 1922 superintendent's mansion, the abandoned Lee Alan Bryant nursing home/mental hospital, and the entire grounds. Self-guided roaming tours are available daily, allowing visitors to explore independently. Flashlight-guided and overnight tours are also offered for those seeking a more immersive experience, providing unique opportunities to spend the night in the hospital's commercial building, the only structure with electricity and water.

While some claim the site is haunted, skeptics may simply find it a thrilling and eerie place to explore, with captivating stories and rumors.

A REAL-LIFE MAYBERRY EXPERIENCE

How is *The Andy Griffith Show* connected to Danville, Indiana?

In a surprising twist, a connection between *The Andy Griffith Show* and Danville, Indiana, exists.

Brad Born, the owner of Mayberry Cafe, has always dreamed of living in a place similar to the fictional town of Mayberry, the show's setting. Brad and his wife, Christine, transformed his dream into reality by opening the Mayberry Cafe in 1989. The café is adorned with floral wallpaper and Brad's extensive collection of memorabilia from the show, creating an ambiance reminiscent of your grandmother's home.

The menu features delectable home-cooked dishes inspired by meals Aunt Bee would serve to Andy and Opie Taylor in the show, transporting diners back in time. In the small Mayberry gift shop, visitors can purchase merchandise, including "Fife for Sheriff" bumper stickers, *Aunt Bee's Mayberry Cookbook*, and Goober hats, allowing them to take a piece of Mayberry home.

Outside the cozy café, visitors are greeted by a replica of Andy Griffith's iconic Ford Galaxie squad car, attracting tourists from all over. It's a popular attraction for photos and likely the most photographed spot in Hendricks County.

Each year in April, the Mayberry Cafe organizes a unique competition called the "Opie Look-A-Like Contest," inviting individuals to showcase their remarkable resemblance to the beloved character Opie.

MAYBERRY CAFE

WHAT: An *Andy Griffith Show*-themed café

WHERE: 78 W Main St., Danville

COST: Varies based on menu prices

PRO TIP: The café is closed on Mondays and tends to be particularly busy on the weekends, resulting in a potential wait.

Notable cast members, including Jim Nabors, Jean Carson, Rodney Dillard Bank, and Maggie Peterson, have graced the café with their presence. Additionally, the daughters of Andy Griffith and Don Knotts make yearly visits to the establishment.

A PERIODIC-TABLE MUSEUM

THE PERIODIC DISPLAY OF THE ELEMENTS MUSEUM

WHAT: 100 individual displays of the elements

WHERE: 602 S College Ave., Percy L. Julian Science & Mathematics Center, Greencastle

COST: Free

PRO TIP: Located on the third floor of the Julian Science Center at DePauw University, just above the staircase.

Why is there thorium on display at DePauw University?

DePauw University in Greencastle houses an extraordinary display known as the Periodic Display of the Elements Museum. Contrary to its name, this exhibit resembles more of a display than a museum. However, with over 100 individual displays of elements, it has earned the title "museum" more than "table." In 2022, this installation graced the third floor of the Julian Science Center through the collaboration of Theodore Gray from Wolfram Research Inc. in Illinois and Max Whitby from the Red Green & Blue Company Ltd. in London.

The periodic table is displayed on a wall and crafted using different wood types, engraved tiles, and unique sample collections. The oxygen display features a quartz slice and zincite samples, while Mercury boasts a vintage mercury thermostat.

Thorium's display includes an intriguing tube of thoriated toothpaste. The pyritized ammonites in the sulfur display and the electrolytic crystal in the copper display will catch your eye.

This table was meticulously designed and constructed with dedication to detail, and it makes an excellent visit for children and science enthusiasts. Visitors can freely explore the display during school hours, although it's less crowded during summer and holiday breaks. Groups are encouraged to contact the school to schedule a visit.

An interactive screen with information about each element and Periodic Table Scavenger Hunt forms are available.

A CHURCH ADORNED WITH TIFFANY GLASS

Which Indiana church boasts a breathtaking collection of Tiffany-glass windows?

In 1906, Richmond industrialist Daniel Reid commissioned the construction of Reid Memorial Presbyterian Church, a Gothic-style limestone church. While its imposing size and striking exterior draw attention, the church's interior is awe-inspiring. Sixty-two stained glass windows, meticulously crafted by New York's renowned Tiffany Studios, adorn the church's interior, making it a treasured landmark. Each window, costing between $2,000 and $3,000 at its creation, contributes to the church's extraordinary beauty. Furthermore, vaulted ceilings, intricate wooden trim, a historic 1906 Boston Hook and Hastings organ, a 1905 Starr concert grand piano, and an elegant bell tower add to the grandeur of the building.

As of 2024, the church was listed on Indiana Landmarks' 10 Most Endangered list. Despite its overall good condition, the church requires repairs estimated to cost over $4 million. To protect and revitalize this historic landmark, the Reid Center aims to transform it into a vibrant cultural and performance venue and serve as an educational and historical destination.

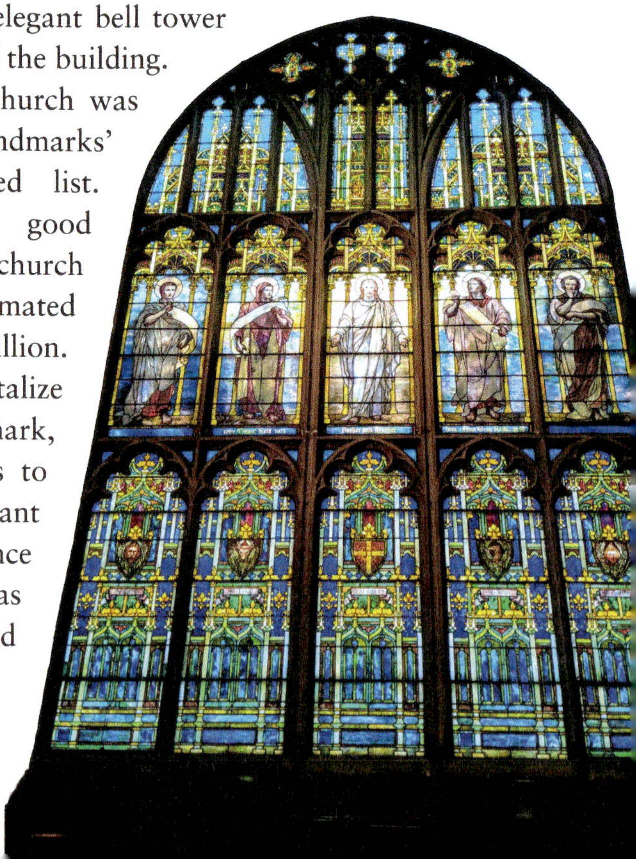

Right: *The historic 1906 Hook and Hastings organ takes center stage inside the Reid Memorial Presbyterian Church.*

When attending a performance at the church, visitors get an immersive experience of the church's rich heritage while it provides a platform for artistic expression and community engagement. Concert attendees can hear the organ or piano played during free and ticketed performances.

REID MEMORIAL PRESBYTERIAN CHURCH

WHAT: A historic church with Tiffany-glass windows

WHERE: 1004 N A St., Richmond

COST: Free, donations are appreciated

PRO TIP: The Reid Center offers free monthly concerts on Wednesdays at noon.

The church was built to memorialize Daniel Reid's parents, Daniel and Ann Gray Reid. The Reids owned a farm in Richmond, near what is now Earlham Cemetery.

A PIZZA SHOP WITH A BUS PARKED INSIDE

CLARA'S PIZZA KING

WHAT: A regional pizza chain with a double-decker bus

WHERE: 1224 NW 5th St., Richmond

COST: Varies based on menu prices (budget-friendly)

PRO TIP: To secure a spot on the double-decker dining bus, call ahead and make a reservation.

How did a double-decker bus get inside the building?

Step into any regional Pizza King, and you will be greeted by its signature Tiffany-style stained-glass lamps, cozy booths, and nostalgic rotary phones at each table. Clara's Pizza King in Richmond offers a unique twist to this familiar ambiance. As you enter, your attention is immediately drawn to the vintage London double-decker bus situated in the heart of the restaurant, preceding the usual accents. This unconventional sight sets this pizza parlor apart from the ordinary.

The intriguing aspect of this building is the double-decker bus nestled within it. This unique design was achieved by constructing the structure around the bus itself. The two-story building offers seating on each level, including a few swings on the top floor for a quirky touch.

Customers can make a reservation in advance to secure a spot on the bus's lower level while they dine. However, it's worth noting that the bus may occasionally be reserved for private parties or events, affecting its availability.

Cement was poured before the Pizza King building was constructed, and the double-decker bus was carefully positioned inside.

Inside the double-decker bus, guests can dine on the lower level.

At Pizza King, customers can take a seat and place their orders using the tableside rotary phone, which they call "ringing the king." When their food is ready, a server promptly delivers it to their table. As Pizza King proudly proclaims, this unique dining experience is "an Indiana thing!"

A WALK AMONG LEGENDS

What famous musicians recorded their music in Richmond?

The Starr Piano Company was founded in 1872 and expanded its offerings to include phonographs and records in 1915. Gennett Records was established as a brand of Starr Piano Co. Gennett Records gained recognition for its groundbreaking recordings of jazz pioneers like Louis Armstrong, Hoagy Carmichael, Jelly Roll Morton, and Duke Ellington, among others. Notably, they also recorded other genres of music featuring artists such as Charley Patton, Gene Autry, and Ernest Stoneman. These recordings were made in Richmond, Indiana, where Gennett Records was based.

The recording studio once stood on the banks of the Whitewater River, but only fragments and the historic Starr Gennett Building endure.

Each medallion has a sponsor, and the accompanying plaque acknowledges the sponsor and includes a dedication message.

GENNETT RECORDS WALK OF FAME

WHAT: A walk of record-shaped plaques honoring music legends

WHERE: 201 S 1st St., Richmond

COST: Free

PRO TIP: If you visit on a Saturday between November and April, you can also visit the Richmond Farmers Market in the historic Starr Gennett Building.

A wide sidewalk leads to Richmond's Whitewater Gorge Park, linking it to the industrial complex site of the Starr Piano Company. Here, record-shaped plaques were crafted to pay tribute to music legends. These plaques form the Gennett Records Walk of Fame, a collection of large ceramic and bronze medallions designed to resemble 78-rpm records, each adorned with the image of an honored artist.

A FOUNTAIN FROM BRAZIL

How did a 62-ton fountain travel 5,000 miles?

In 1950, the country of Brazil bestowed a diplomatic gesture of friendship upon its namesake, the City of Brazil in Indiana: a magnificent gift in the form of an entire fountain. This remarkable fountain, known as the Chafariz Dos Contos or "Fountain of Tales," is a replica of the fountain in Ouro Preto, Brazil, constructed between 1724 and 1760.

The fountain, sculpted by artist Tito Bernucci, weighs 62 tons. The brick and granite fountain was packed into 104 crates and shipped across 5,000 miles. Its voyage began by ship, carrying the fountain to Baltimore, where it then continued its journey inland by rail, ultimately arriving in Indiana. The assembly process, which took three years and cost $13,000, resulted in a magnificent structure that stands 26 feet tall and spans approximately 40 feet in length.

Over time, the fountain fell into disrepair, but it underwent two extensive restoration projects. In 1997 it received a restoration and rededication, and between 2016 and 2020 a comprehensive four-year restoration took place. This latest restoration included replacing the stucco, applying new paint, repairing the roof and fountain basin, and rebuilding the water system to restore the fountain's gurgling waters.

In 2022 three flagpoles were installed at the fountain, representing the United States, the state of Indiana, and Brazil, further enhancing its significance as a symbol of international friendship and cultural exchange.

The Chafariz Dos Contos, or "Fountain of Tales," is a tribute to and captures the historical significance of the original fountain in Brazil.

CHAFARIZ DOS CONTOS

WHAT: A 62-ton replica fountain from Brazil

WHERE: Forest Park, 911 Bonnie Geyne Miller Dr., Brazil

COST: Free

PRO TIP: The fountain is at the entrance of Forest Park, across from the baseball diamonds, and next to a picnic pavilion and playground.

AN EIGHT-SIDED HOUSE

Why did Jane build an octagon-shaped home?

Only five octagon houses remain in Indiana, including the Jane Ross Reeves Octagon House in Shirley. However, the house did not initially reside there. Before relocating to Shirley in 1997, it stood between Wilkinson and Willow Branch, Indiana.

On their initial farm, Jane and Elijah Reeves built a log cabin. However, three years after her husband's passing in 1879, Jane replaced it with the Octagon House. The inspiration for this two-story, octagon-shaped home came from a magazine featuring the design of Orson S. Fowler. He believed this unique shape promoted better health by allowing increased airflow and sunlight. For the house's construction Jane hired Trehr and Brewster, a company based in Fortville, Indiana. The construction cost was around $2,500, which Jane surprisingly paid in full using silver dollars she had saved in a shoebox.

JANE ROSS REEVES OCTAGON HOUSE

WHAT: One of the last remaining octagon homes in the state

WHERE: 400 S Railroad St., Shirley

COST: Free

PRO TIP: The Octagon House is open to the public for private tours by request or during events.

The Octagon House, known for its architectural features, has 16 rooms, each with a unique triangle-shaped closet. This design accommodated the large Reeves family, as Jane had 12

This Octagon House is the most significant of the five remaining in Indiana since it has never been altered except for adding a porch. It was listed on the National Register of Historic Places in 2001.

children. The house featured a central staircase and four chimneys positioned to serve two rooms each, both upstairs and downstairs.

After Jane's passing in 1907, the Octagon House remained within the Reeves family until its abandonment in the 1970s. During this period of disrepair, a group of dedicated men from Shirley stepped forward to relocate and restore the house to its former glory.

A TREE-MENDOUS COURTHOUSE CURIOSITY

Why is there a tree on this courthouse's roof?

In the middle of Decatur County, Greensburg hides a peculiar sight—a tree poking out of the courthouse roof. In the 1820s, Greensburg, the county seat of Decatur County, constructed its first county buildings in the courtyard. Decades later, in the 1870s, locals discovered a peculiar sight atop the courthouse. Initially it was just a small sprig, but over time it grew into a small tree firmly rooted in the crevices of the tower roof. It's like Mother Nature was having a bit of fun, rooting it in the cracks of the tower roof.

Before long, four additional shoots began to sprout, raising concerns among officials about the damage they could inflict on the roof. In response,

The iconic Tower Tree, featured on an episode of *Ripley's Believe It or Not*, continues to captivate minds as an unsolved oddity.

THE TOWER TREE

WHAT: A courthouse tower with a tree growing through it

WHERE: 101–199 N Franklin St., Greensburg

COST: Free

PRO TIP: While you're at the Courthouse Square, a historic spot in its own right, take some time to explore the historic sites around it.

they removed some of the shrubs from the building. One tree, however, survived for many years before dying and being relocated to the Decatur County Historical Society Museum. However, the story didn't end there. Another tree emerged on the tower's southeast corner and another on the southwest corner. Those two mulberry trees keep growing strong on the tower's roof, making the county courthouse even more famous.

The Tower Tree stands tall and proud, showing off its colorful leaves during the fall. It's a sight to behold, leaving everyone in awe. But how those seeds got up on the tower roof is anyone's guess. It's a mystery that keeps people wondering and guessing.

COURTHOUSE WITH A *STAR TREK* CONNECTION

BOONE COUNTY CIRCUIT COURTHOUSE

WHAT: County courthouse with the world's largest columns

WHERE: 310 Courthouse Square, Lebanon

COST: Free

PRO TIP: The courthouse is open on weekdays, and visitors must pass a security check, so don't bring prohibited items.

Which courthouse blends grandeur, artistry, and a touch of Hollywood?

In 1911, architect Joseph T. Hutton designed the Neoclassical-style courthouse in Boone County, featuring the world's largest single-piece limestone columns. The courthouse is surrounded by eight monolithic limestone columns, each over 35 feet tall and weighing approximately 30 tons. The columns are made from rough-cut blocks of stone shipped from Bedford, Indiana, and refined on-site before being hoisted to the courthouse's entryways.

The courthouse's monolithic columns, standing over 35 feet tall and weighing approximately 30 tons each, are the world's largest single-piece limestone columns.

The building's main feature is the courthouse's captivating centerpiece, the magnificent stained-glass dome column. With a diameter of 52 feet, this architectural marvel towers 84 feet above the ground. The dome's design features an octagonal art-glass dome, adding grandeur. Its hues and patterns dance with the sunlight, casting kaleidoscopic reflections on the interior walls below. The dome is ranked the second-largest in the state, surpassed only by the iconic dome of the West Baden Springs Hotel in French Lick.

Since its construction, the majestic courthouse has been featured in the news multiple times. One peculiar incident occurred in 2001 when William Shatner and his fourth wife visited the courthouse to obtain and pay a $62 out-of-state residence fee for a marriage license. This amusing anecdote adds a touch of Hollywood glamour to the courthouse's history and amuses *Star Trek* fans.

Aside from its extraordinary columns and dome, the courthouse has other notable features. The building has white Italian marble, green Vermont cable, and several rooms with 1-¼-inch quartered oak.

WONDERS OF THE NIGHT SKY

Where can you find a hidden gem for stargazers and astronomy enthusiasts?

Prairie Grass Observatory (PGO) is a haven for stargazers and astronomy enthusiasts—and no one seems to know it exists! At Camp Cullom, a nonprofit youth camp under dark rural skies, PGO offers an array of instruments for exploring the wonders of the night sky. Propelled by donations and dreams, this observatory opened in 2001.

PRAIRIE GRASS OBSERVATORY AT CAMP CULLOM

WHAT: Campground with an observatory

WHERE: 6815 W Co. Rd. 200 N, Frankfort

COST: Free

PRO TIP: While Camp Cullom is open daily, the observatory is open to the public only during events.

Visitors to PGO can choose from four telescopes to observe celestial objects: a colossal 28-inch aperture Dobsonian, a 16-inch LX200R Schmidt-Cassegrain telescope (known for its role in asteroid discoveries), a 16-inch Newtonian telescope, and a 7-inch apochromatic refractor.

In addition to these featured telescopes, PGO boasts a pair of giant 25/40×100 binoculars and a hydrogen-alpha filter, enabling visitors to observe the sun safely. To enhance the viewing experience, the observatory has wide eye-relief

The PGO is named for its location amid one of the largest expanses of native prairie grass in the state.

eyepieces, cameras, and projectors, allowing individuals or groups to explore the night sky in detail.

While it may be described as "small," this hidden gem, tucked away in Indiana, offers a stellar experience. The observatory hosts free events throughout the year, such as the Indiana Family Star Party and Open House evenings, allowing visitors to immerse themselves in astronomy and use the telescopes. Families can come together to learn about the wonders of the night sky, participate in hands-on activities, and marvel at the stars and planets through high-powered telescopes. During Open House evenings, the observatory opens its doors to the public, allowing visitors to explore the facility and meet with experts.

INDIANA'S SLEEPY HOLLOW

Is the Sleepy Hollow Bridge haunted, or are these tales just folklore?

Legend has it that in the 1800s, a woman committed a heinous act: she murdered her husband, loaded his body onto a wagon, and disposed of it in the South Fork Wildcat Creek beneath the bridge. This dark secret haunted her until her dying day. Another urban legend describes a tragic incident in which a school bus full of children was struck by a train on an adjacent track, resulting in a devastating outcome.

Despite these tales, some locals claim they've never witnessed anything unusual near the bridge. However, others embellish the stories, adding their eerie accounts. The true nature of Sleepy Hollow Bridge's legends may remain a mystery, but it remains an obscure site for curious visitors seeking a glimpse into the unknown realm.

The Sleepy Hollow Bridge has undergone renovations, resulting in a more modern appearance, unlike its eerie

Locals have varying opinions on the authenticity of the legends, with some claiming never to have witnessed anything unusual and others embellishing the stories.

CLINTON COUNTY'S SLEEPY HOLLOW

WHAT: A bridge with urban tales

WHERE: N Co. Rd. 580 W (40°19'14.4"N 86°36'48.5" W), Mulberry

COST: Free

PRO TIP: Sleepy Hollow is near the cemetery on the paved North County Road 580 West. It's easily mistaken for the older bridge on the adjacent gravel road.

ambiance in the 1800s. Initially, it was an old metal truss bridge, replaced with a newer structure. Just down the road lies a historic cemetery; however, it's on private property and inaccessible to visitors. Despite its inaccessibility, the cemetery's presence enhances the mystery surrounding the Sleepy Hollow Bridge. One can't help but wonder about the stories hidden beneath the ground, the lives that once intersected here, and the secrets that may forever remain concealed.

Although the Sleepy Hollow Bridge may not emit the same eerie aura today as it did in the 19th century, it continues to attract individuals seeking paranormal encounters.

VAULT DINING EXPERIENCE

Where can you dine inside a bank vault and historical landmark?

Located in Huntingburg's historic old bank building, Butcher and Barrel restaurant offers an unparalleled fine dining experience within the walls of a historic landmark. The three owners, driven by lifelong friendship and a love for the area, returned to Huntingburg to raise their families and share their passion for barbecue.

Its grandeur is evident in the soaring 20-foot ceilings and the mezzanine dining area that provides a sweeping vista of downtown Huntingburg. However, the true gem of this establishment lies in its unique dining spaces. Patrons can choose to dine in the former bank vault, now transformed into an intimate and exclusive dining area for two. This unique space adds a touch of history and intrigue to any dining experience. The vault's thick concrete and steel walls still feature a small porthole, a reminder of a past incident where the former owner was accidentally locked inside while working late. This quirky detail serves as a conversation starter and a testament to the building's rich history.

Butcher and Barrel's ambiance is uniquely enhanced by the impressive floor-to-ceiling bookcase behind the bourbon

bar, showcasing an extensive collection of over 150 varieties of bourbon, scotch, and Irish whiskeys. The warm glow and rich bourbon aroma permeate the air, complemented by the authentic Bourbon Barrel Staves that adorn the walkway, host stand, and bar area. These thoughtful touches create an inviting and sophisticated atmosphere, making Butcher and Barrel a must-visit destination for food enthusiasts and history buffs.

BUTCHER AND BARREL

WHAT: Restaurant in former bank building with vault dining

WHERE: 416 E 4th St., Huntingburg

COST: Varies based on menu prices

PRO TIP: It is recommended that you make reservations online, especially for the vault dining experience.

The restaurant resides in a nearly 100-year-old bank building listed on the National Register of Historic Buildings.

THE GRAVE WITH LIPSTICK KISSES

Why are there lipstick kisses on this rebel's grave?

Fairmount is the small home town of iconic American actor James Dean, who was raised there following his mother's passing. Renowned for his heartthrob status in 1950s Hollywood, Dean's notable roles include *Rebel Without a Cause*, *East of Eden*, and *Giant*. His untimely death at the age of 24 in a high-speed car accident further solidified his legendary status.

In the small town of Fairmount, the James Dean Gallery and Museum, memorial, and annual festival bring out enthusiasts of the iconic actor. However, it's surprising that few know he is also buried in Fairmount. His gravesite is a peek into the mysteries of his life. Dean's final resting place lies in Park Cemetery, near his childhood home. Finding his gravesite might pose a challenge, as his tombstone is modest and unassuming, reading simply: "James B. Dean, 1931–1955." The original headstone had to be replaced several times due to theft. Adjacent to his gravesite, his father, aunt, and uncle are also buried.

JAMES DEAN GRAVE

WHAT: The gravesite of rebel heartthrob James Dean

WHERE: 8106–8334 S 150 E, Fairmount

COST: Free

PRO TIP: Follow the signage provided to locate James Dean's burial site. It is situated just off the lane atop a small hill.

Outside the glitz and glam of Hollywood, Dean was known for his rebellious nature, further enhancing the status that surrounded him.

At Dean's gravesite, a plethora of tributes are left by his devoted admirers. His headstone, adorned with countless lipstick kisses, is a testament to his enduring appeal as a young heartthrob. Visitors often leave coins, such as pennies, nickels, dimes, and quarters, bearing the year of Dean's untimely passing. Cigarettes, guitar picks, Hot Wheels cars, and other memorabilia associated with the star's iconic legacy are frequently left behind as tokens of remembrance.

THE GOLDFISH CAPITAL OF THE WORLD

Why is Martinsville known for being the goldfish capital?

OZARK FISHERIES

WHAT: The goldfish capital of the world

WHERE: 2353 N Ozark Fisheries Dr., Martinsville

COST: Fee for admission

PRO TIP: Group tours must be reserved in advance based on farm availability. Additionally, closed-toe shoes are required for safety.

Have you ever imagined Indiana as the "Goldfish Capital of the World"? I hadn't either. However, Indiana's treasures hold delightful, quirky, and odd experiences.

In 1899, Eugene Shireman established Grassyfork Fisheries. As goldfish gained popularity in the United States, Shireman ventured into fish farming on swampy land he had inherited in Martinsville, Indiana. He bought 200 goldfish for breeding and began operations in 1902. Grassyfork Fisheries blossomed into one of the largest hatcheries globally.

In the 1920s, the popularity of goldfish experienced a significant surge, primarily driven by the establishment of pet departments in chain stores. During this period, the United States was home to more than 60 goldfish producers, indicating the scale and demand for these pets.

Photo courtesy of Ozark Fisheries

Photos courtesy of Ozark Fisheries

Ozark Fisheries acquired the hatchery in 1970, continuing its operations on the 1,100-acre farm, selling millions of fish yearly. The Martinsville location is one of the oldest continuously operating fish farms in the United States, producing goldfish and koi. Group tours are available upon request for school, FFA, and community groups. As Ozark Fisheries is a working farm, all tours must be reserved in advance. Tours are a hands-on experience, immersing oneself in the farm's history and exploring the hatchery and facilities.

The historic Grassyfork office building was listed on the National Register of Historic Places in 2012 and restored by a local businessman.

A FOOTWEAR FORTRESS

How did this castle become a footwear store?

Driving through downtown North Webster, Indiana, you can't miss this castle-like structure. Although North Webster doesn't have a bustling downtown, the "Castle" stands out in this small town. This is precisely what banker J. Homer Shoop intended when he built the Castle in 1967 to attract more tourists. In 1971 he demolished his bank building and used the block (which he named "Camelot Square") to construct a castle-like building for a sports museum.

The Castle opened in 1972 as the International Palace of Sports. It was a unique combination of tourist attraction and kitsch, unlike any museum the Hoosier State had ever seen. Inside the museum, a pool propelled jets of water from three fountains. The second floor led visitors to "The Royal Gallery of the Realm of Recreation." The museum hosted a gift shop and an odd wax figure gallery named "Kingdoms of Sport." Even more extravagant was a full-sized tennis court located on the roof. Notable sports personalities such as O. J. Simpson, Jesse Owens, Pancho Gonzalez, Johnny Weissmuller, and Dick Weber have graced the museum with their presence.

After Shoop sold the museum in 1979, it rapidly declined and closed in 1989. The museum's contents were dispersed through an auction. The Pilcher family subsequently acquired

the expansive Castle and transformed it into the largest shoe store in the Midwest, which remains in operation. Additionally, the River Coffeehouse has established a presence within the Castle, allowing visitors to indulge in coffee and shoe shopping in this bizarre, historic building.

PILCHER'S SHOES

WHAT: A castle structure built as a sports museum

WHERE: 127 S Main, North Webster

COST: Free to visit; varies based on purchases

PRO TIP: If you need shoes, Pilcher's has over 100,000 pairs of men's sizes 5–20, women's sizes 4–13, and widths ranging from 4A to 14E.

Homer Shoop, a prominent citizen of North Webster, was a sports enthusiast, amateur tennis player, banker, and castle-builder.

THE LEGACY OF LAKE WEBSTER

THE *DIXIE* STERNBOAT

WHAT: Indiana's oldest sternwheel excursion boat

WHERE: 127 S Main St., North Webster

COST: Fee for admission

PRO TIP: Public cruises are offered from Memorial Day to Labor Day. Each cruise lasts 75 minutes and is wheelchair accessible.

Can a steamboat be an early version of Instacart?

In 1914 Joseph Breeck constructed the inaugural *Dixie* sternboat in Madison, Indiana. He had a cottage on a tiny island in Webster Lake called Breeck's Island (now called Dixie Island) and property known as Dixie Camp. In that era, the area was relatively unpopulated, and Breeck's boats offered services to residents requiring mail and grocery delivery around the lake. It might be considered an early-1900s version of Instacart.

By 1928, the original *Dixie* was nearing the end of its lifespan, prompting Breeck to construct a new boat with a steel hull. He repurposed components from the old boat to build cottages and a pilot house for the new *Dixie* vessel. The new *Dixie* resembled its predecessor and made its first voyage in 1929.

Before 1982, Dixie Camp was a modest resort and campground featuring seven vintage 1920s rental cabins and a sternwheel vessel for excursions. The new owner removed the old cabins and introduced modern motel units, a restaurant with a scenic lake view, and a spacious boardwalk.

Breeck retired in 1939, selling the *Dixie* and its property to Jay Knapp, the *Dixie*'s captain. Knapp maintained the boat's operations until 1949 when he sold it to Earl Ungeright. Ungeright preserved the *Dixie*'s legacy by upgrading and operating it for over 22 years. In 1955 the *Dixie* briefly served as a Showboat Production stage.

In 1981 the Dixie Camp underwent a significant renovation and a change of ownership. The *Dixie* boat had been dry-docked since 1966. In 2007, it was transferred to Dixie Sternwheeler, Inc., a 501(c) nonprofit organization, and continues to operate as a tour boat.

A SLICE OF HORROR

Where can you dine amongst horror movie legends?

Max Miller, a passionate collector of classic monster-movie memorabilia for over five decades, drew inspiration from his hobby to establish Famous Monster Pizza in downtown Decatur in 2018. This locally owned and operated pizza shop is a testament to Miller's love for monster movies. The establishment is decorated with an array of monster-related collector's items, including magazines, posters, books, toys, and more, creating a unique and captivating ambiance.

The pizza shop's theme and decor pay homage to the iconic monsters that graced the silver screen from the early to late 20th century. The dining area is transformed into a fun and frightful setting, with classic monster movies playing on big screens and adjustable drive-in movie speakers at each table. This experience allows patrons to enjoy their pizza while immersing themselves in the thrilling world of classic monster cinema.

At the entrance of Famous Monster Pizza, you are greeted by a soda fountain and eerie familiar characters, such as Pennywise and E. T., lurking about. Inside, you'll find Dracula lounging in a coffin, surrounded by memorabilia-

FAMOUS MONSTER PIZZA

WHAT: A horror movie-themed pizza restaurant

WHERE: 136 N 2nd St., Decatur

COST: Varies based on menu prices (budget-friendly)

PRO TIP: It's best to visit early, especially on the weekends, since it's a popular place.

At times, Famous Monster Pizza hosts celebrities from horror films and shows, including Butch Patrick who played Eddie Munster on the television series *The Munsters*.

covered walls. The restaurant's location is rich in history. The south building, built in 1883 as the First National Bank, retains many original features. The north building served as the Cort Movie Theatre from 1930 to 1956.

Beyond its "frightful" atmosphere, Famous Monster Pizza offers a monstrously themed menu with Transylvania Deep Dish or Frankenstein pizza, a 21-inch Big Monster Grinder, mummy rolls, and more. You can order drinks and desserts from their Old Fashion Soda Fountain, such as Dr. Jekyll's Marshmallow Cola or a Zombie Milkshake. It's a menu that is sure to "die" for.

GAMING INSIDE AN OLD LIBRARY

Why does this old library building feature a dragon statue?

Venture into TCB Games, as "The Collectors Box Games" is called for short, and be greeted by a life-sized wizard known as "Draconis the Enlightened One." Rows upon rows of video games, board games, comics, and collectibles will surround you. This business isn't just a hobby store; it's an organization that aims to foster connections through games. Descend to the lower level and discover a dedicated gaming area. Here, individuals can gather to enjoy games or participate in Magic Gatherings.

TCB Games stands out as distinctive to Huntington. Occupying the old Huntington Public Library, it captivates the attention of passersby with its iconic dragon statue mascot, "Charlie," protruding from the building's side. Charlie holds a special significance, as he is named after the owner's childhood imaginary friend, inspiring the company's logo and the statue itself.

Its building rescued from potential destruction, TCB Games has preserved the original layout and design. It features rows of shelves reminiscent of a library, now proudly displaying a diverse collection of items for sale. Ascending the stairs leads to an upstairs balcony, where rows of comics and movies beckon enthusiasts.

On the building's main level, customers can discover an extensive array of video games, consoles, and role-playing games. Board games, disc golf equipment, collectibles, and craft model-building sets are also available. Snacks and cold beverages are conveniently available for those who plan to stay and play. Additionally, the establishment provides gaming system repair services.

TCB GAMES

WHAT: A premier gaming store inside an old library

WHERE: 44 E Park Dr., Huntington

COST: Free to visit; varies based on purchases

PRO TIP: Bring your games and game consoles if you want to sell or trade them in.

TCB Games offers the convenience of a seven-day-a-week operation, including extended evening hours.

AN EXCAVATED SUNKEN OASIS

How did an abandoned quarry turn into a garden destination?

Sometime in the 1910s, the Keefer and Biley Lime, Brick, Tile, and Cement Company abandoned their quarry in Huntington, leaving an unsightly scar on the city's landscape. In response, construction of the Sunken Gardens began in 1923, transforming the abandoned quarry into a beautiful and vibrant public space. Inspired by a similar quarry sunken garden in San Antonio, the city had set its sights on a fresh location for a community park.

The Chicago Landscape Company designed the 1.5-acre site, incorporating footbridges, fountains, fieldstone staircases, and a horseshoe-shaped pool. The project took six years to complete. Limestone and original stonework from the old quarry created garden features, including limestone walls, entrances, and a fieldstone bridge. The natural walls form a living

HUNTINGTON SUNKEN GARDENS

WHAT: A historic park and sunken gardens complex

WHERE: 1125 W Park Dr., Huntington

COST: Free

PRO TIP: Pack a picnic and enjoy the playground, disc golf, basketball and tennis courts, and scenic walking trails surrounding the gardens.

The Sunken Gardens is in Memorial Park, which houses a remarkable Veteran's Memorial.

amphitheater, making the gardens popular for weddings and annual holiday light displays.

Surrounded by ponds, walkways, bridges, colorful flowers, and lush foliage, the Sunken Gardens create a breathtaking setting for events and casual visitors alike. An accessible path allows individuals of all abilities to enjoy the gardens' natural beauty and tranquility. It's a unique example of transforming an unsightly area into a beautiful and functional space, and it remains one of only two such gardens in the country.

A STUFFED DOG FROM 1900

Why is a taxidermied dog displayed at the Huntington County Historical Museum?

Have you ever encountered a taxidermied dog, especially one from the late 1800s? If not, then the weird tale of Old Sully may fascinate you.

During the decade between 1890 and 1900, Old Sully was affectionately known as the "town dog" throughout Huntington. Every day, he would eagerly wait for the children to be dismissed from Horace Mann School, his favorite hangout spot. Old Sully's nature made him loved by everyone, particularly the children. As he roamed the streets for companionship, business owners often treated him to snacks. Old Sully's owner, George Reynolds, allowed him to roam freely, and one of his frequent destinations was Sumner Bash's residence for breakfast.

In 1900, Old Sully got into a fight with another dog, sustaining injuries that forced him to limp back to his owner, George. Despite George's efforts to clean and bandage his wounds, the faithful companion laid down on his favorite bed and quietly passed away. Recognizing the children's love for Old Sully, George had him stuffed and preserved, donating him to the school. From there, Old Sully's preserved remains resided at the museum of the old Carnegie Library, later being stored in an attic. A few years later, the library board president discovered him and had him put back on display.

Huntington is known for its odd history, including the row of old outhouses on the museum's property.

OLD SULLY, THE DOG

WHAT: A taxidermied dog from 1900

WHERE: Huntington County Historical Museum, 315 Court St., Huntington

COST: Free

PRO TIP: Old Sully is located at the front of the museum.

Old Sully's presence at the library proved unsettling for many visitors, so he was relocated to the Huntington County Historical Society museum, where he remains on display.

THE EERIE ANTIQUE SHOP

SHABBY OWL ANTIQUES

WHAT: A haunted antique shop and Airbnb

WHERE: 107 N Walnut St., North Manchester

COST: Free to visit; varies based on purchase prices

PRO TIP: The antique shop is open only on Saturdays and accepts only cash or checks. You can call in advance to schedule a time to browse their store on other days.

What mysterious pasts do these antiques hold?

Hidden above the Shabby Owl Antiques shop is a unique Airbnb rental that caught my attention. With its quirky and eerie atmosphere, the entire building exudes a spooky vibe. Little did I know that the discovery of this Airbnb would lead me to a curious antique shop located on the lower level.

Both the antique shop and Airbnb are in the historic Pythias building. In the past, the Knights of Pythias held secretive meetings within its walls. Thousands of antiques can be found inside the store and the Airbnb—it's quite a unique experience. Despite the eerie feeling of being watched, visiting either location promises a range of activities to engage your mind. Given the building's rich history and the countless

historic items that have passed through it, it's no wonder that paranormal enthusiasts are drawn to this mystical place.

The owners have reported unexplained occurrences within the building, including objects mysteriously falling off walls, personal items being tampered with, and items being moved unexplainably in the antique shop. These activities permeate the entire structure, encompassing the antique shop, wood shop, and Airbnb. The eclectic and enigmatic Airbnb features access to the former Knights of Pythias ballroom, now adorned with interesting taxidermy, an embalming table, and unsettling dolls.

If you're seeking an unconventional shopping experience, Shabby Owl Antiques is that. Along with its vintage taxidermy, the shop has an array of more ordinary and fascinating antiques, including vintage wooden furniture, primitives, farmhouse goods, architectural salvage, boutique items, industrial goods, and jewelry. But if you're searching for a stuffed raccoon, pig, skull, creepy doll, or mannequin, you'll find that here, too.

In the past, the Knights of Pythias owned the historic Pythias building, where they conducted secret meetings behind its walls.

A CANAL WITH IRISH HERITAGE

What is the connection between the Irish and Kerr Lock?

In the early 1800s, a wave of Irish immigrants seeking economic opportunities arrived in Lagro. The demand for faster and more efficient westward travel led to the popularity of canal construction, attracting many Irish workers to canal-digging jobs. Despite the hard labor and long hours, the pay was good, with workers earning around $13 monthly, equivalent to a year's rent.

The Wabash Erie Canal was completed in 1843 and experienced its peak activity in the 1850s. It was a transportation route for merchant boats traveling between Fort Wayne and other destinations. The Kerr Lock, a hand-operated lock system, was built in Lagro and played an important role in regulating the canal's water level. The lock was constructed from stone procured from the local Salamonie quarry and was wide enough to accommodate one boat at a time.

By the 1870s, canals were abandoned for the faster and more efficient railroad network. While the Kerr Lock and remnants of the Wabash-Erie Canal remain visible in Lagro, the canal's passing marked a period of decline. Many businesses relocated, and the villages waned as employees of the canal and its related industries sought opportunities elsewhere.

KERR LOCK HISTORICAL MONUMENT

WHAT: A historic site with remnants of Kerr Lock

WHERE: 610 Washington St., Lagro

COST: Free

PRO TIP: To find the Kerr Lock historic site, look for the historical marker, Kerr Lock sign, and historic cabin.

Despite the canal's demise, the Irish heritage in Wabash County continues. Only one original dwelling remains from the small housing settlement that accommodated the first Irish immigrants working on the canals, built around 1835. Today, this one-room canal house, known as the Riparian House, serves as an Airbnb. St. Patrick's Catholic Church, constructed for the Irish laborers who helped dig the canal, still stands. Although it is no longer an active church, Mass is held at the site once a month, and it's a beautiful building visit.

Little evidence of the canal system in Wabash remains, except for the Kerr Locks in Lagro, the lock remnants near Richvalley, and the rear doors on south Canal Street buildings that faced the canal docks.

SPLINTERS FROM THE CROSS

What museum claims to have two splinters from the cross on which Jesus was crucified?

The Cathedral of the Immaculate Conception in Fort Wayne dates back to 1859. It's a gorgeous historical building with impressive wood carvings and stained glass. The Diocesan Museum is attached and filled with hundreds of religious artifacts, some dating back to the time of Jesus Christ and Abraham. Father Phillip Widmann opened the museum in 1981, attracting Catholic and non-Catholic visitors.

Within the walls of the museum are displays dedicated to the history of the Catholic faith and religious artifacts. Many of these items are significant to the Diocese of Fort Wayne-South Bend. Visitors can see some of the oldest and most intriguing religious artifacts, including a handwritten Bible dating back to the mid-13th century, relics belonging to St. Mother Teresa and St. Elizabeth Ann Seton, a collection of nun dolls, and an 85-year-old statue portraying the graphic wounds of Jesus.

The most astonishing artifact is a display that purportedly holds wood slivers from the cross on which Jesus Christ was crucified. The two slivers are arranged in the shape of a cross and stored in a sealed container. According to historical accounts, St. Helena discovered these wood slivers in Jerusalem in 326 AD, and they were later retrieved from the Persians in 629 AD. While

---

The museum's artifacts mainly originate from Father Phillip Widmann's collection. He spent over four decades collecting, restoring, and rescuing abandoned items from local churches that had closed. Additional artifacts have been donated to the museum.

a display card acknowledges the skepticism surrounding St. Helena's discovery, the Church celebrates the Triumph of the Holy Cross each year.

DIOCESAN MUSEUM

WHAT: A Catholic museum with historic artifacts

WHERE: 1103 Calhoun St., Fort Wayne

COST: Free

PRO TIP: Free parking is available in all cathedral parking areas.

Photos courtesy of Visit Fort Wayne

INDIANA'S "GRAND CANYON"

Where can you watch limestone being blown up?

In Fort Wayne lies a hidden gem: the Hanson Quarry, often called "Indiana's Grand Canyon." A secret viewing deck offers visitors an expansive and unobstructed view of this magnificent quarry. The quarry's history dates back to the early 1900s when it was established for sand and gravel extraction. However, in the 1950s, operations transitioned to limestone, coinciding with the construction of the observation tower.

Heidelberg Materials Company owns the quarry called "Indiana's Grand Canyon." Despite being a captivating attraction for locals and tourists for several decades, it remains an undiscovered treasure. The quarry is accessible to the public at no charge, with daily visiting hours from dawn to dusk.

Located along Sand Point Road, the Heidelberg Materials Company's vibrant yellow building is a landmark for finding the tower. The observation tower offers a unique opportunity

HANSON QUARRY OBSERVATION TOWER

WHAT: An observation deck overlooking a 1900s quarry

WHERE: 4529 Sand Point Rd., Fort Wayne

COST: Free

PRO TIP: The gates are open from sunrise until sunset. Before visiting, confirm that the location is not renovating, as this may result in temporary closures.

Every day, the Hanson limestone quarry's 1,000-foot-deep hole sinks deeper into the earth's surface.

for curious onlookers to witness the spectacle of giant excavating machines ripping through solid limestone. Visitors can observe blasts being executed within the quarry from a safe vantage point. This display elevates the art of excavation and demolition to an entirely new level, ensuring both thrill and safety. The limestone extracted from this quarry is used for buildings, homes, sidewalks, and other projects throughout Fort Wayne and beyond.

LETTERS FROM LINCOLN

What's inside the world's largest collection of Lincoln artifacts?

Inside the Allen County Public Library lies a remarkable collection of original artifacts associated with President Abraham Lincoln—the most extensive such collection in the world! The library contains over 20,000 Lincoln items. In 2022, the library unveiled the Rolland Center for Lincoln Research, an immersive and interactive space showcasing priceless Lincoln Financial Foundation Collection items. The Friends of the Lincoln Collection supported this center, which has helped preserve and present President Lincoln's legacy for generations.

The Rolland Center is near the Plaza entrance of the Great Hall in the Main Library. It is open to the public and offers an immersive experience, allowing visitors to explore physical artifacts on display and engage with virtual items through innovative tech elements. The Center's goal is to create a connection between people and Abraham Lincoln's life and times. The displays showcase an unparalleled collection of Lincoln-related materials, including unique items that make this one of the most impressive collections of presidential artifacts I've seen in the state.

Two Lincoln librarians are on staff at the library, and their expertise and familiarity with the Lincoln Collection were invaluable while organizing the materials and developing storylines for the exhibit.

Photos courtesy of Visit Fort Wayne

THE ROLLAND CENTER AT ALLEN COUNTY PUBLIC LIBRARY

WHAT: The world's largest collection of Lincoln artifacts

WHERE: 900 Library Plaza, Fort Wayne

COST: Free

PRO TIP: The Rolland Center is open whenever the library is open.

The exhibit includes original photographs of Abraham Lincoln, his family, Cabinet members, and generals. It also contains letters and documents written to and from Lincoln, diaries of soldiers from the Civil War, and other artifacts. The displays provide an overview of Lincoln's life, including his role as a lawyer and legislator, the elections he participated in, and slavery including the Emancipation Proclamation. Furthermore, the Lincoln family album offers a glimpse into his personal life and relationships.

MONSTER-TRUCK MANIA

What's the most monstrous attraction in Butler?

Only in Butler, Indiana, could you occasionally find something pretty wild—a gigantic monster truck cruising through town! It's not unusual for residents, as Butler is home to the International Monster Truck Museum (IMTM) & Hall of Fame. Unmissable, right outside the museum, is a monster-truck billboard featuring a hollowed-out frame of a 1987 Chevrolet pickup truck. Nicknamed the Sky Rider, the truck lacks an engine and transmission but sits atop towering 80x55 tires.

This museum is one of a kind, dedicated to the thrilling world of monster trucks. It has everything from old-school trucks to modern beasts, like the legendary King Kong and the colossal Goliath. And it's not just about the trucks—you'll also find memorabilia, like driver uniforms, crew shirts, and historic body panels. Truck legends, pioneers, and fans have donated items to the museum to use in displays. It has a rotating schedule of over six classic monster trucks that

Photos courtesy of International Monster Truck Museum & Hall of Fame

you can check out up close and personal. It is interactive, too, with displays designed to teach kids about monster trucks and their history.

The International Monster Truck Museum & Hall of Fame was started in 2010 to celebrate the history of monster trucks and the people who made them what they are today. The museum honors the sport's pioneers and legends annually by inducting them into its Hall of Fame.

INTERNATIONAL MONSTER TRUCK MUSEUM & HALL OF FAME

WHAT: A monster-truck museum

WHERE: 541 W Main St., Butler

COST: Fee for admission

PRO TIP: While in the area, check out the Auburn Cord Duesenberg Automobile Museum and National Auto & Truck Museum in nearby Auburn, Indiana.

The IMTM frequently organizes events throughout the year, allowing attendees to experience monster-truck rides and witness them in action as they roll through town.

A SANCTUARY OF HEALING THROUGH WATER

KNEIPP SPRINGS AT OUR LADY, PATRONESS OF AMERICA CENTER

WHAT: Historic property with a healing water spring

WHERE: 2730 E Northport Rd., Rome City

COST: Free

PRO TIP: Bring bottles to fill up with water from the three-spigot water fountain, which is just feet from the actual source of the artesian spring and flows naturally.

What is the connection between the "Kneipp Cure" and Rome City?

Throughout its history, Kneipp Springs, also known as Kneipp Sanatorium, served as a destination for individuals seeking the "Kneipp Cure." This approach aimed to prevent or cure illnesses using hydrotherapy from the natural mineral springs. In the 1880s, Dr. Sebastian Kneipp, a priest, philosopher, and advocate for natural healing, formulated the Kneipp Cure. This approach sought to promote overall well-being through hydrotherapy, emphasizing natural foods, exercise, and herbal teas. His 1886 book, *My Water Cure*, became an international bestseller.

Dr. W. Giermann, a physician trained in Vienna to use water cures for medicinal purposes, established the Kneipp Sanatorium to facilitate the application of the Kneipp Cure.

The Kneipp Sanatorium was a destination for individuals seeking to prevent or cure illnesses using hydrotherapy from healing natural springs.

From the natural spring, there's a three-spigot water fountain accessible to the public at no cost.

At its peak, Kneipp Springs boasted over 20 buildings and functioned as a working farm with orchards. For decades, the facility welcomed over 1,500 visitors annually.

In 1901, the Sisters of the Precious Blood visited Kneipp Springs and purchased it from Dr. Giermann the following year. Their goal was to establish a sanctuary for the sick and needy, continue the sanatorium's purpose, and practice charity. The Sisters maintained the resort's operations until the 1970s. Patients seeking medical treatment resided on-site in the spacious spa building or nearby outbuildings. Stays could range from a month to years, with many patients suffering from chronic physical or mental illnesses.

In 2018, Kneipp Springs was recognized as the Kneipp Springs Historic District on the National Register of Historic Places. While some buildings remain under renovation, the renovated chapel, now known as Our Lady, Patroness of America Center, hosts Mass. Property tours are offered three days a week, and visitors continue to visit Kneipp Springs for its therapeutic waters. The spring's refreshing water flows continuously from a fountain, providing free access to the public. Having personally tasted it, I can attest to its natural properties.

A TREASURE TROVE OF AMERICAN ART

Who houses hand-signed lithography by Norman Rockwell?

Known for its vibrant arts and jazz culture, Elkhart boasts the most extensive collection of hand-signed lithographs by the renowned American painter and illustrator Norman Rockwell. In the heart of downtown, the Midwest Museum of American Art (MMAA) stands tall, housed in an elegantly renovated 1920s neo-classical-style bank building. The original circular vault door, preserved as a unique architectural element, is an intriguing entrance to one of the museum's galleries.

Across the street from Hotel Elkhart, the museum houses a permanent collection of over 6,000 artworks, some displayed within the hotel itself. Daily, visitors can admire around 1,200

MIDWEST MUSEUM OF AMERICAN ART

WHAT: 19th through 21st century, nonprofit art museum

WHERE: 429 S Main St., Elkhart

COST: Fee to visit

PRO TIP: Admission is half-off every Thursday for Noontime Talks.

pieces representing the United States' artistic heritage, notably featuring the work of historic Indiana artists.

Among the notable artists whose works grace the museum's collection is Rockwell, a prolific artist with over 4,000 artworks to his credit and a regular contributor to the *Saturday Evening Post*. The MMAA has the most extensive collection of Rockwell's signed and numbered, limited-edition collotypes and stone lithographs.

In addition to Rockwell's pieces, the museum showcases original works by Grant Wood, Overbeck Art Pottery, abstract expressionism, Chicago imagists, and American impressionism, offering diverse artistic styles and perspectives.

The Midwest Museum of American Art was founded in 1979 by Dr. Richard and Jane Burns.

BEHIND-THE-CURTAIN TOUR

What treasures await in this backstage exploration?

In downtown Elkhart, the Lerner Theatre, formerly the ELCO Theatre, showcases an Adamesque architectural style with four two-story ionic columns and three grand arches. The ornate multi-colored marble floors, domed ceiling, a colossal chandelier, and a balcony complete the theater's grandeur.

Opened on Thanksgiving Day in 1924, the Lerner Theatre accommodated 2,000 patrons. The theater has a rare treasure: a 1924 Kimball pipe organ, one of only three installed in its original location. This organ is regularly used for organ concerts and silent movie screenings, allowing audiences to experience a bygone era.

THE LERNER THEATRE

WHAT: Historic theater tours

WHERE: 410 S Main St., Elkhart

COST: Fee for tour

PRO TIP: To schedule a 45-minute guided tour, call 574-293-4469 to make your reservation.

Like many historic structures, the Lerner is associated with an urban legend. This legend originates from the unfortunate demise of a tech director who succumbed to a heart attack while

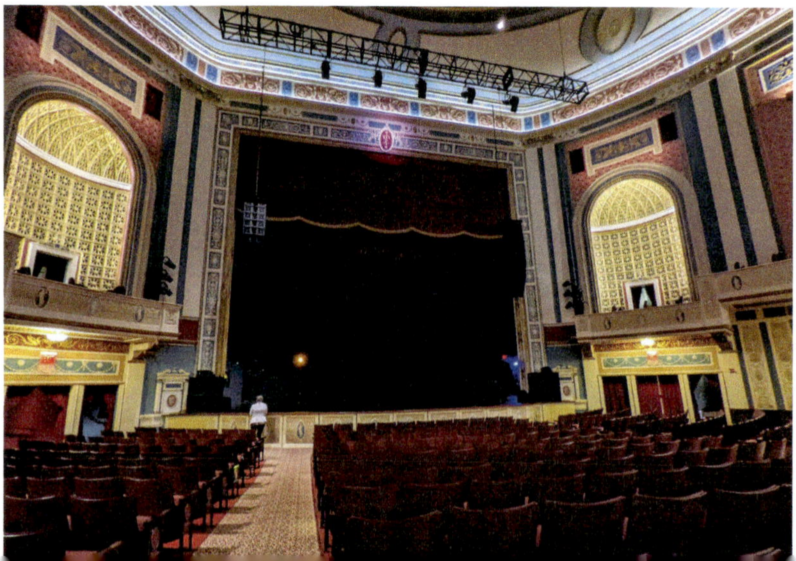

The Lerner's Crystal Ballroom features crystal chandeliers, elegant draperies, and a balcony overlooking Central Park and Downtown Elkhart.

on duty. Visitors can explore the theater through guided tours that delve into the history of the Lerner and its significant individuals, offering glimpses of its architecture and providing a backstage perspective. Expert tour guides lead the way, sharing captivating tales of the theater's construction, architectural marvels, and the legendary performers who have graced its stage. The theater has even hosted specialized haunted-history tours, immersing participants in a mystical experience.

Whether you opt for a tour, attend an organ concert, or witness a show, you will be captivated by the theater's magnificent features.

In 2008 the theater was renovated to restore its original splendor. The ceiling and signature "mushroom" chandelier were meticulously hand-painted over several weeks.

THE RV AND TRAILER CAPITAL OF THE WORLD

RV/MH MUSEUM & HALL OF FAME

WHAT: An RV and mobile-home museum

WHERE: 21565 Executive Pkwy., Elkhart

COST: Fee for admission

PRO TIP: The parking lot accommodates RVs with pull-through spaces for vehicles up to 65 feet long.

Where can I find the world's only RV/MH museum?

In Elkhart County, Indiana, known as the "RV and Trailer Capital of the World," an RV/MH Museum and Hall of Fame seems perfectly fitting. Notably, Elkhart County produces over 80 percent of the world's RVs, and in 1948 it earned the title of "Trailer Capital of the World." Many RV and manufactured homeowners' cherished vehicles likely originated in Elkhart. While the concept of an RV/MH museum may initially sound unconventional, it serves as a haven for enthusiasts and owners of these mobile accommodations.

"RV/MH" is an abbreviation for "Recreational Vehicle and Manufactured Housing." The museum has multiple sections that showcase the history and significance of RVs and manufactured homes. These sections include the RV Founders Hall, the RV/MH Exhibitors Hall, the Scoular MH Museum, and the Go RVing Hall. In addition to these exhibits, the museum houses the Kindlund RV/MH Library, the only library solely dedicated to the RV and MH industries. Its extensive collection includes thousands of periodicals and records.

The RV Founders Hall exhibit showcases trailers and memorabilia from the 1920s to the present. In the Go RVing exhibit, visitors explore a collection of modern and luxurious recreational vehicles and campers.

In 2022, the Scoular MH Museum joined forces with the RV Museum, merging their efforts to honor and preserve the rich

history of the manufactured housing industry. This museum section takes visitors on a journey through time, beginning with the covered wagon and progressing through each decade from the 1930s to the 1980s. Immersive interactive displays bring the past to life, while a dedicated children's play area is designed for ages 3–5.

The RV/MH Museum and Hall of Fame is a tribute to the nomadic lifestyle and attracts seasoned travelers and curious first-timers.

THE SUBMARINE SECRETS OF LAKE MICHIGAN

Who was the daring 20-year-old who navigated the Great Lakes in a submarine?

Lake Michigan's mysteries and beauty have captivated Hoosier residents for centuries, and a compelling history is closely tied to the lake. Among the state's historical landmarks is Michigan City's Old Lighthouse Museum, which opened in 1973. The museum's significant architecture and association with lake transportation earned it a spot on the National Register of Historic Places. While Michigan City's marine history is well-known, its submarine story is relatively forgotten.

Within the museum's walls are seven exhibit rooms, each telling a maritime and local history story. Among the artifacts is a submarine model, a replica of the first to navigate the Great Lakes. You read that right, a submarine on Lake Michigan.

OLD LIGHTHOUSE MUSEUM

WHAT: Display of Lake Michigan's first-ever submarine.

WHERE: 100 Heisman Harbor, Michigan City

COST: Fee for admission

PRO TIP: Check hours in advance; winter hours are more limited.

In 1845, an innovator named Lodner Darvontis Phillips, then only 20 years old, unleashed his invention upon the waters of Lake Michigan. His submarine, "Fool Killer," mirrored the mindset of that era, where any craft designed to submerge beneath the water was deemed a fool, sure to result in death. Phillips crafted his submarine with both salvage and warfare in mind. His cigar-shaped design laid the groundwork for the basic structure adopted by the Navy's early submarines. While his initial submarine was unsuccessful, in 1851, he embarked on an all-day trip beneath the surface of Lake Michigan in a revised submarine, accompanied by his family.

Several of Phillips's submarines either rest at the bottom of the lake or are unaccounted for. G. C. Calvert meticulously crafted a 1:1 scale model of the 1851 submarine using surviving drawings of Phillips's. This model and replicas of Phillips's three patents are on display at the Old Lighthouse Museum.

The museum is located directly opposite the site where Lodner Phillips triumphantly launched the first Great Lakes submarine in 1845.

THE SOLITARY COLUMNS

What's the story behind the old columns in front of the Horizon Building?

Horizon Bank has a deep history in Michigan City, dating back to 1857. Initially known as the First National Bank, it received its charter in April 1873. While visiting Michigan City, I stumbled upon these old limestone columns in front of the Horizon Building. Upon finding this oddity, I felt compelled to investigate further. Through research, I uncovered the history behind these solitary columns, which appear out of place.

In 1873, Walter Vail arrived in Michigan City to establish the First National Bank with a capital of $50,000. He purchased a property on Franklin Street and started operations on the second floor of his newly acquired building. As the bank expanded, it moved to the Odd Fellow's Building in 1878, then to the Leeds Building in 1903, and finally to its new building at 515 Franklin Street. After Vail's passing, J. F. Kriedler assumed the role of president in 1911, followed by William W. Vail, the founder's son, in 1916.

The original First National Bank building was demolished in 1975 to make way for the construction of the First-Merchants National Bank. This merger resulted from the union between First National Bank and Merchants National Bank in 1962. Later, a merger

FIRST NATIONAL BANK COLUMNS

WHAT: Historic column remnants

WHERE: 515 Franklin St., Michigan City

COST: Free

PRO TIP: The columns are within a few miles of the historic Old Lighthouse Museum in Michigan City.

The impressive columns outside the bank's current headquarters in Michigan City are a testament to the building's past.

with Citizen's Bank led to the formation of First Citizens Bank, which was subsequently renamed Horizon Bank in 1997.

Today, the portico columns of the former First National Bank building stand prominently in the heart of the city, in front of the Horizon Building. These columns were constructed in 1920, which is evident from the inscription "First National Bank, 1920" etched along their top.

THE "POOR MAN'S HARVARD" CHAPEL

Which university holds the largest college chapel in the United States?

Throughout its over 160-year existence, Valparaiso University has undergone three distinct phases. It was founded in 1859 by Methodists as the Valparaiso Male and Female College, one of the first coeducation institutes in the United States. However, the setbacks of the Civil War forced it to close its doors in 1871. In 1873, educator Henry Baker Brown revived the institution as the Northern Indiana Normal School. Later, in 1900, it was renamed Valparaiso College and then Valparaiso University in 1906.

Right: *Adjacent to the chapel, the August H. and Ella Louise Brandt Campanile houses 12 bells that chime throughout the day.*

These stunning works of the country's largest college chapel's beauty are a powerful reminder of the faith and history that shape the Valparaiso community.

VALPARAISO UNIVERSITY CHAPEL OF RESURRECTION

WHAT: The largest college chapel in the country

WHERE: 1600 Chapel Dr., Valparaiso

COST: Free

PRO TIP: In front of the chapel are an unusually shaped labyrinth and a pretty prayer garden.

Over the next two decades, the university established business and law schools, gaining national recognition as a low-cost institution for higher learning, dubbed "the Poor Man's Harvard."

Despite its success, Valparaiso University faced financial challenges during World War I. In 1925, the Lutheran University Association purchased the university, marking the beginning of Valpo's modern era.

In 1956, Valpo's chapel-auditorium was destroyed by a devastating fire. Three years later, it was replaced by the majestic Chapel of the Resurrection. Standing at 98 feet tall, this is the largest college chapel in the United States. Situated on the highest elevation of Valparaiso's campus, its circular shape is topped by a magnificent nine-pointed star and adorned with 95-foot-high stained-glass windows, known as the Munderloh Windows. Designed by renowned German artist Peter Dohmen, these windows were donated by a couple in Detroit, Michigan.

A FERRIS-WHEEL TALE

DUNN'S BRIDGE

WHAT: Bridge built from the World's Fair Ferris-wheel scrap

WHERE: 500 E over the Kankakee River, Kouts

COST: Free

PRO TIP: Dunn's Bridge is always visible and accessible from dawn to dusk. It is located just west of the road. On the north side there is a pull-off spot for parking and a boat launch.

Which piece of iconic fair history might be hiding in an unassuming Indiana bridge?

Before discovering the history of Dunn's Bridge, I never imagined that a small-town bridge could harbor such intriguing rumors and heritage. Spanning 180 feet across the Kankakee River, Dunn's Bridge was initially constructed by Indiana farmer J. D. Dunn using scrap metal from an exceptional source—the world's first Ferris wheel. However, some say the bridge was built in the mid-1890s using steel beams salvaged from the 1893 Columbian Exposition in Chicago. Others suggest that the bridge was constructed using pieces of the original Ferris wheel, which debuted at the fair and was later dismantled after the 1904 World's Fair. In 1994, the Porter County Parks Department acquired and restored the bridge, earning it a prestigious place on the National Register of Historic Places.

While most historians acknowledge that the Hoosier farmer built the bridge, its exact details remain a mystery. Porter County did purchase the bridge and three surrounding acres, establishing the Dunn's Bridge County Park. This historic landmark holds exceptional value as a piece of county history and serves as a gateway to unique environmental features in the area. Ultimately, the truth behind the Ferris-wheel legend remains a matter of individual interpretation. You can visit the bridge and see if you can spot remnants of the rumored Ferris-wheel scrap, as the legend originated from many sources.

Results from metal tests indicate that the steel used in the construction of Dunn's Bridge originated from the same foundry responsible for casting the iconic first Ferris wheel.

ECHOES OF THE PAST

What stories do the walls of the 100-year-old Buckley Barn whisper?

Buckley Homestead, a 575-acre living-history farm, has been under the watchful care of Lake County Parks since 1983. Originating in Ireland, the Buckleys immigrated to the United States in the mid-18th century. In 1849, their journey brought them to Northwest Indiana, where they settled and established their first farmstead. Visitors can find live animals, an old-fashioned schoolhouse, and the historic Buckley Barn, which is over 100 years old and has earned the entire homestead a spot on the National Register of Historic Places. Before researching for this book, I was unfamiliar with the existence of the Buckley Homestead.

As a living history farm, Buckley Homestead operates as both a park and a historical venue. The main areas of interest within the homestead are the barnyard, the house, and the live animals. The cabin is furnished as it would have been during the 1910 era, providing a glimpse into the past and the hard life of farming. A pioneer farm at the back of the

BUCKLEY HOMESTEAD

WHAT: An 1849 living-history farm

WHERE: 3606 Belshaw Rd., Lowell

COST: Free

PRO TIP: The park is accessible from 7 a.m. until sunset throughout the year. However, the historic buildings have seasonal operating hours.

Each year, the homestead organizes a Headless Horseman event, drawing inspiration from similar events at Conner Prairie. However, it is more affordable, making it accessible to a broader audience.

Photos courtesy of South Shore CVA

property represents the 1850s, and the schoolhouse area reflects the period from 1880 to 1910.

During a visit to the Buckley Homestead, a conversation with the park employees may reveal some fascinating facts. In the 1800s and 1900s, lilac bushes were planted for various purposes. One of these purposes was to mark the grave of a miscarriage or the place where the placenta was buried after birth. However, a less honorable purpose was to plant them near outhouses to reduce unpleasant odors.

THE MASS-PRODUCED MARVEL

How did a shiny chromium alloy ignite automotive success?

Elwood Haynes, an inventor and resident of Kokomo, made history by becoming the first person to mass-produce automobiles commercially. His former mansion now serves as the Elwood Haynes Museum, preserving his legacy. Despite his significant contributions to modern motoring, Haynes remains relatively underappreciated compared to other notable figures in the automotive industry.

Haynes's journey took him to Kokomo, where he built the first automobile and discovered an alloy of pure chromium. Here, he invented the "Horseless Carriage," a gasoline-powered automobile. He designed and funded it and drove the first commercially built auto in the country. In 1898, he began producing automobiles under the Haynes Apperson logo, leaving a lasting mark on the automotive industry.

Born in Portland, Indiana, Elwood Haynes attended college in Massachusetts, where he discovered tungsten chrome steel.

But his contributions didn't end there. He was also named the "Father of the Natural Gas Industry" in Indiana. Haynes invented the vapor thermostat, which regulates heat in homes. He also served as the superintendent of the Indiana Natural Gas Company in 1890.

The museum is a time capsule for history and car buffs. It features Haynes Model automobiles, including the 1923 Haynes Speedster. Additionally, the museum pays homage to other groundbreaking inventions and "firsts" that have made Kokomo renowned. My favorite exhibit is the adjacent carriage house, where visitors can peer through the expansive garage windows and marvel at the very first automobiles produced in Kokomo.

ELWOOD HAYNES MUSEUM

WHAT: The museum for the first commercial auto-producer

WHERE: 1915 S Webster St., Kokomo

COST: Free, donations accepted

PRO TIP: A narrow driveway leads to parking in the back of the house, which is unsuitable for larger vehicles like buses or RVs.

WHERE FICTION MEETS SNACKS

What is the "story" of this convenience store in Kokomo?

In Kokomo, fiction intersects with snacks at the Storybook Express Drive-Thru. This unexpected yet charming convenience store was constructed in 2012 to help revitalize the downtown area. It defies conventional expectations.

Scott Pitcher of Fortune Companies, Inc., describes it as "whimsical in nature." Its architectural design captures the attention of passersby and those with an imagination. In front of the store, a storybook retaining wall materializes the theme, with shards of colored glass emerging from the concrete slabs at odd angles.

The "fairy tale" structure is not just a uniquely themed work of art but also environmentally conscious and recycled. The materials used for the brick building, stone detailing, and walls were repurposed from old Indiana schools and a demolished local fire station. Adding to its whimsy, various antiques can be found throughout the exterior. A bowling ball is embedded within the wall, a metal pig's posterior sits in the wood above the transom window, and a big fake electrical outlet is on the side of the building.

The Storybook draws significant attention due to its unique appearance. It's not common to encounter a shop resembling a "Harry Potter house" during a typical drive through town.

The other sides of the building offer a convenient drive-through, revealing more hidden antiques within the wall, such as a car's suspension coil, antiquated plumbing fixtures, and an old church inscription reading "Enter Into His Courts With Praise." In contrast to its whimsical exterior, the interior resembles a regular convenience store, offering drinks, snacks, and the convenience of a drive-through window.

In keeping with the storybook theme, the windows and decor are artfully angled, creating an illusion. The glass in the walls originates from Kokomo Opalescent Glass, a renowned local glassmaker.

STORYBOOK EXPRESS DRIVE-THRU

WHAT: A storybook-themed convenience store

WHERE: 316 E Sycamore St., Kokomo

COST: Free to visit; varies based on purchase prices

PRO TIP: Another Kokomo building by the same builder has a similar storybook architecture. It is at the intersection of Markland Avenue and Calumet Street.

THE PRESERVED PAIR

What's the oddest couple in Highland Park?

In 1902, Kokomo experienced an unusual event. A calf named Old Ben, weighing an astounding 125 pounds at birth, made his appearance. Old Ben grew into the world's largest steer, capturing the attention of circus owners and sideshow representatives eager to acquire him. However, his owners declined these offers, instead showcasing him in a private tent at fairs throughout Indiana, including several appearances at the Indiana State Fair.

Tragically, a broken leg led to Old Ben's demise in 1910. The beef from the world's largest steer was made into frankfurters, while the owners had him stuffed and preserved. At his death, Old Ben weighed between 4,585 and 4,720 pounds, stood 6.5 feet tall, and measured 16.25 feet long from nose to tail. Old Ben's legacy lives on, as he was featured in Ripley's "Believe It Or Not" in 1968 and now resides in a pavilion at Highland Park.

SYCAMORE STUMP AND OLD BEN

WHAT: A historic tree stump and the world's largest stuffed steer

WHERE: 1402 Defenbaugh St., Kokomo

COST: Free

PRO TIP: These roadside attractions in Highland Park are surrounded by nature, playgrounds, and picnic areas. It's a great picnic stop for travelers to Kokomo.

Visitors to Highland Park can glimpse Old Ben's stuffed figure, displayed alongside the iconic Sycamore Stump behind glass in the park's visitor center. This weird combination offers not one but two unusual roadside attractions.

Once standing tall at the west end of Howard County, the Sycamore Stump reached a height of 100 feet before being taken down by storms, leaving behind a huge, hollow stump. Its trunk boasted a circumference of over 50 feet, and it is estimated to be between 800 and 1,500 years old, but no one really knows. The stump was relocated to Highland Park in 1916, where it continues to be displayed beside Old Ben.

THE BIG-TOP LEGACY

Who's ready to step into the ring of Peru's circus legacy?

Ladies and gentlemen, and children of all ages . . .

With a rich circus heritage dating back to the late 19th century, the circus has been a beloved part of Peru, Indiana, for over a century. One can't miss the iconic big top (now home to the Peru Amateur Circus) near the town's heart when visiting Peru.

Maria Rasputin, daughter of the notorious Grigori Rasputin, traveled from Paris to Peru in 1935 to join the then-Hagenbeck-Wallace Circus. Her father, known as the "Ma Monk," was a Russian mystic and faith healer who gained fame for his friendship with the imperial family. However, he met a tragic end when Russian nobles conspired to assassinate him several times, cementing his legendary status. Maria capitalized on her father's notoriety by re-enacting his legendary death, which drew international attention. Unfortunately, her circus career in Peru was cut short after several bears attacked her.

Today, the circus is still alive in Peru. In July, they host an annual eight-day extravaganza, including the Circus City Festival and the world's longest-running circus parade (one of Indiana's largest parades). Around 200 people participate in the circus performances. Notably, many performers from Peru

have showcased their talents with renowned circuses such as Ringling Bros. Barnum & Bailey and Shrine Circuses.

The city of Peru is also home to the International Circus Hall of Fame and the Circus City Museum, which preserves the history of the circus. The International Circus Hall of Fame is housed in five original circus winter quarters buildings constructed by the American Circus Corporation in 1922. These buildings contain historic circus wagons and artifacts and have been designated as National Historic Landmarks. Visitors can walk through both locations and explore displays, wagons, artifacts, circus costumes from the past, photos, and miniatures.

CIRCUS CITY MUSEUM

WHAT: A circus museum

WHERE: 154 N Broadway, Peru

COST: Free by donation

PRO TIP: Situated within the Circus City Center, the Circus City Museum operates during office hours from August to February. The Circus Hall of Fame, located at a different site, is open from May through February, with an admission fee.

The International Circus Hall of Fame offers camping for tents and RVs. Campers can set up on the historic circus grounds that lions, tigers, and elephants once called home.

PILLARS OF TIME

How did the Miami people utilize this sacred site?

Along the Mississinewa River in Peru lies a hidden gem known as the Seven Pillars of the Mississinewa Landmark. This natural wonder, located within the Seven Pillars Nature Preserve, consists of seven 25-foot limestone pillars. Over the centuries, erosion has sculpted these pillars, creating alcove-like chambers between each one.

The land holds sacred significance for the Miami people and is protected by the ACRES Land Trust. Before and during early contact with Europeans and Americans, the tribe frequently utilized the alcove rooms within the formation for council meetings and other activities. At one point, a trading post operated from the site. The tribe revered the pillars as a "gateway to the other world," believing the place was abundant with spirits traveling between realms. The site hosted ceremonial dances, victory feasts, and Long House ceremonies. French Catholic traders reportedly experienced unsettling encounters with spirits at the site, leading to its reputation for being haunted.

SEVEN PILLARS OF THE MISSISSINEWA LANDMARK

WHAT: A geological wonder on the Mississinewa River

WHERE: 3985 Mississinewa Rd., Peru

COST: Free

PRO TIP: For the best view of the Seven Pillars, head to the southern bank of the river, accessible from Mississinewa Road.

The Miami Nation of Indians of Indiana continues to gather at the Seven Pillars of the Mississinewa Landmark for Long House ceremonies and their annual Miami Heritage Days at the Pillars.

Hikers can take the Frances Slocum Trail, which runs along the top of the Pillars, reaching heights up to 50 feet above the river. This 25-mile trail stretches from Marion to Peru, allowing for entry at various points along its length.

THE CABIN WITHIN A HOUSE

How was the Blann Cabin discovered?

THE HISTORIC BLANN CABIN

WHAT: A historic log cabin

WHERE: Corner of SR 41 and SR 114, Morocco

COST: Free

PRO TIP: The cabin is located at the rear of the Newton County Government Building.

In a remarkable discovery, a concealed treasure, the Blann Cabin, was found inside another home, like stacked Chinese nesting dolls. Records indicate that John Dimmitt acquired the land the house stood on under the Swamp Land Act of 1852 and was the cabin's earliest known owner. In May 1878, John sold the property to his partner, George McMurchey, and his wife for a symbolic $1. Fifteen subsequent owners held the log cabin before it was acquired from the US Marshal as a result of a railroad lawsuit.

Ultimately, the Blann family became the owners in the early 1900s. However, in 2004, they sold the property to a land developer. Unbeknownst to the developer, an extraordinary artifact lay concealed within a house on the property.

Photo courtesy of Firkins Film

Photo courtesy of Firkins Film

While dismantling the house, the developer stumbled upon an immaculately hand-built 1-½ story log cabin in pristine condition, nestled within the larger home.

The cabin was relocated to the grounds of the Newton County Government Center in Morocco, Indiana, as per the developer's agreement. The cabin is considered Newton County's oldest structure and stands alone along a pond, accessible via a small gravel road. Visitors can drive to the cabin and admire its exterior, including a hand-built stone chimney. The roof had to be replaced in 2020 due to deterioration, and although it's not the original roof, it will keep the cabin protected from elements to preserve it for the future.

While the log cabin's original history remains somewhat a mystery, it is believed to date back to the 1850s when Dimmitt acquired the land, approximately 20 years after white Europeans settled along the Iroquois River in northwest Indiana.

AN INTERGALACTIC VOYAGE

Where can one walk around the sun without leaving Earth?

In West Lafayette, Indiana, at Purdue University's Discovery Park, an interactive, walk-through sculpture called the VOSS Model showcases the vastness of our solar system. Designed by artist Jeff Laramore and Purdue students, this $1.5-million exhibit spans the length of a football field.

The centerpiece of the VOSS Model is the "sun," a 45-foot-diameter sphere surrounded by marble planets set in 6-foot-high walls. Each planet orbits the sun, putting the size of space into perspective. In contrast, the Earth model is a mere 6 inches wide. At night, the planets illuminate, creating a very cool display.

The VOSS Model is based on the Fibonacci Spiral, a mathematical pattern that recreates the logarithmic spiral found in nature. For every step taken around the sculpture, one travels 5.4 million miles in space.

The VOSS Model is dedicated to Purdue alumnus Janice Voss, an engineer and NASA astronaut who logged over 48 days in space, flying on three missions and mapping over 47 million square miles of Earth's land surface. A trailblazer, she was one of only six women to have gone to space five times. Voss passed away at the age of 55 after a brave battle with breast cancer.

This unique piece of art allows visitors to appreciate the beauty and scale of our solar system. The VOSS Model is a testament to Purdue University and its students' creativity and is dedicated to astronaut Janice Voss.

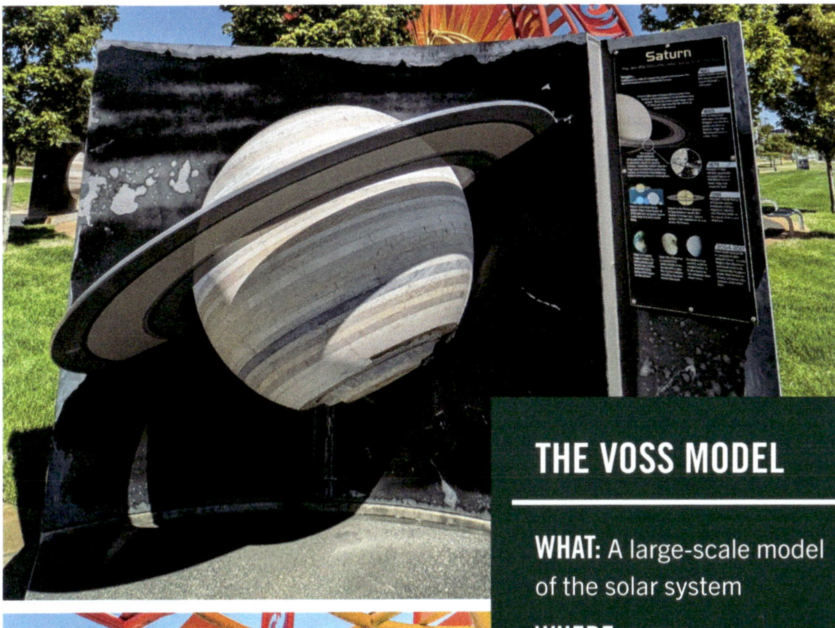

THE VOSS MODEL

WHAT: A large-scale model of the solar system

WHERE: 217 S Martin Jischke Dr., West Lafayette

COST: Free

PRO TIP: Free and metered street parking is located around Discovery Park.

THE GAS STATION TRANSFORMATION

How did a 1927 gas station become a 24/7 library?

The Standard Oil Company of Indiana built a gas station in Lafayette in 1927. The building had a one-garage bay attached, featuring glazed brick walls and a red tile roof. In 1935 the station added a second garage bay. The gas station operated as Jonesy's Stand Oil station until 1979. In 1985, the library acquired the property for future parking.

A local businessman and auto collector generously offered to restore the gas station, and the restoration project was completed in 1992. The restored building's interior and exterior were filled with gas station memorabilia, primarily related to Standard and Red Crown Gasoline, while the garage bays housed antique cars. Over time, the vehicles and most of the memorabilia have been removed, leaving the historic building to serve as a unique space for the new 24-hour library.

The Red Crown Mini-Museum, now home to the Tippecanoe County 24-hour library, stands at the corner of 6th and South Streets in downtown Lafayette, Indiana, adjacent to the Tippecanoe County Library.

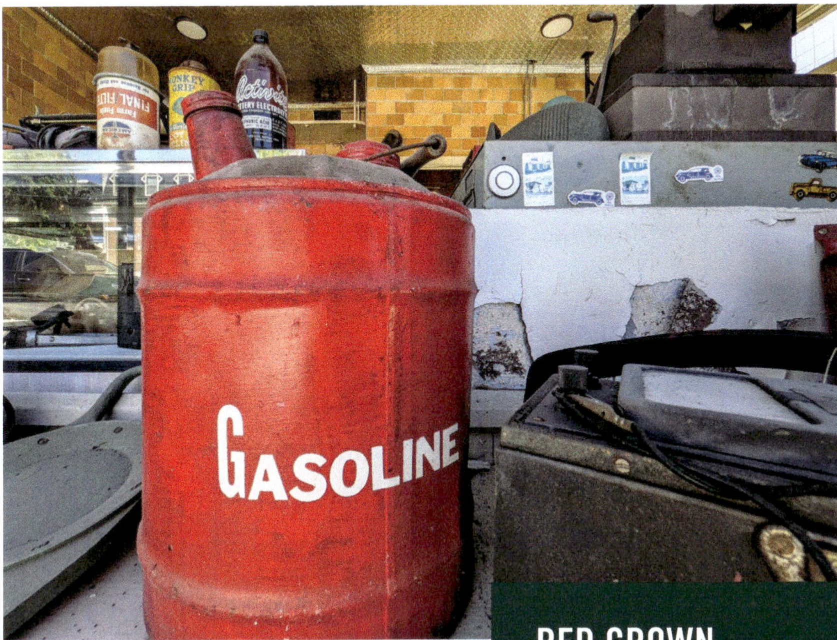

In December 2018, the Tippecanoe County Library unveiled a 24-hour library within the renovated Red Crown Mini-Museum. This distinctive library resembles a large ATM and houses a collection of 300 books, audiobooks, and movies. In 2023, the building underwent further renovations, and a greenscape was added to enhance the library's surroundings.

RED CROWN MINI-MUSEUM

WHAT: Historic filling station

WHERE: 605 South St., Lafayette

COST: Free

PRO TIP: The former museum is part of the library system, but visitors can drive or walk up to see it anytime.

WALL OF MURALS

Why is this city section covered in murals?

Driving through Lafayette, I stumbled upon a city section with vibrant murals. These beautiful artworks lined businesses, warehouses, and even residential homes. Historically considered a marginalized area, Wabash Avenue is a working-class neighborhood often referred to as the "lower part" of town and holds remnants of a bygone era. Its reputation has endured challenges over the decades. What was once a hidden enclave along the Wabash River has been transformed into a radiant cultural hub, largely thanks to the "Wabash Walls" initiative. The murals, known as the Wabash Walls murals, are a creative initiative undertaken by the Arts Federation (TAF) and a collaborative educational outreach initiative that enhances the quality of life for marginalized individuals and communities.

WABASH WALLS

WHAT: A neighborhood of murals

WHERE: Wabash Ave., Lafayette

COST: Free

PRO TIP: The TAF website has a map of all the murals throughout Lafayette and the state.

In 2008, the Wabash Walls program was established to revitalize communities across 14 North Central Indiana counties that TAF served. Initially piloted in Lafayette, the program aimed to reduce vandalism and has since transformed this region into an artistic hub.

Boundaries Are in Your Mind *mural by artist Juegasiempre.*

The program's success lies in partnering local community members with talented artists to develop themes, content, and subject matter that resonate with the specific population.

The Conductor *mural by Cobre.*

Firefly *mural by Max Sansing and* Fiddle *by Jenna Morello.*

Artists worldwide have contributed their skills and creativity to various communities in North Central Indiana, leaving a lasting impact on the region.

The Arts Federation annually presents the Wabash Walls Festival, the first mural festival in Indiana.

THE WHISPERING WINDMILLS

What sets this windmill museum apart from others?

In Indiana, towering windmill farms may stir controversy, but Kendallville presents a delightful contrast with its unique windmill gathering and wind-power education. In the Midwest, where the wind whips and whispers, the Mid-America Windmill Museum and Historical Society tells the tale of American wind power the best.

Established in 1992, the museum preserves and celebrates the history of American windmills. Over 50 restored American water-pumping windmills grace the museum's barn and a gravel walking path. Visitors can get up close to them, see model windmills, and learn about the barn's history on site. Outside, the antique windmills sway in the breeze, their blades creaking and groaning, creating an eerie "windmill song" that echoes through the air.

These windmills serve as educational tools, raising awareness of the evolution of American windmill power from its inception to the present day. One museum highlight is the replica of the original Robertson Post Windmill, shipped from England in the 1620s. Made of

MID-AMERICA WINDMILL MUSEUM

WHAT: An American windmill museum

WHERE: 732 S Allen Chapel Rd., Kendallville

COST: Fee for admission

PRO TIP: Guided and self-guided tours are available, and the museum is mostly outdoors, so check the weather in advance.

The Mid-America Windmill Museum and Historical Society offers a glimpse into American windmills' history and significance.

Top photo is courtesy of Jamie McCann. Bottom photos are courtesy of Visit Noble County Indiana

stone and wood, this 52-foot-diameter grist mill is a testament to the early days of windmill technology. Additionally, the museum showcases models of windmills produced by the Flint & Walling Company from 1870 to the mid-1950s. It's the only museum to house all 11 models in its collection.

WORSHIP ON THE WATER

WAWASEE BOAT-IN

WHAT: Largest waterborne worship service

WHERE: Oakwood Resort & Conference Center, 702 E Lake View Rd., Syracuse

COST: Free

PRO TIP: Afterward, you can grab coffee or breakfast at Oakwood's restaurant and coffee shop. Seating is free on the SS *Lillypad*, but first-come, first-served.

Why does this congregation wear bathing suits to church?

On summer Sunday mornings, a chorus of voices echoes across Lake Wawasee, Indiana's largest natural lake. People gather for the off-shore Wawasee Boat-In, a Christian non-denominational worship service from Memorial Day through Labor Day, hosted by Compass, a ministry of the Syracuse-Wawasee Ministerial Association. Boats and the shoreline become the congregation, harmoniously blending spirituality and the lake's natural beauty. It's a breathtaking experience.

Worshippers arrive by boat or gather on the shore at Oakwood Resort & Conference Center in Syracuse for the 30-minute services. You do not need to be

an Oakwood guest to attend the service; it is open to everyone. Even the SS *Lillypad*, a 70-foot dinner houseboat, joins in, offering free rides from the Frog Tavern to the service.

On a nearby pier, speakers diffuse music over the lake, inviting everyone to join in for praise and worship. Attendees dress casually in shorts, tank tops, flip-flops, and sometimes even bathing suits, reflecting the relaxed and casual lake setting. These boat-in services testify to the versatility of church practice, reminding us that the "house of God" can exist anywhere, even on and within the water.

In the 1990s, Harlan Steffen launched Boat-In, and the gatherings drew hundreds to thousands of attendees, making it the largest waterborne worship service and earning recognition from the *New York Times*. Donations from Boat-In are dedicated to funding Compass, a compassionate ministry, which relies solely on volunteers. The funds serve as a lifeline for individuals and families in need within the Wawasee Lakes area.

Boat-in services are held throughout the region at several surrounding lakes, a tradition that has been ongoing for decades.

Photo courtesy of Wawasee Compass

THE UNLIKELY HOME OF A TEAM STORE

What do baseball and a synagogue have in common?

The South Bend Cubs are a minor-league baseball team in South Bend, an affiliate of the Chicago Cubs. While the team is well known in the region, its team store has an intriguing history that sets it apart from other stores.

Once known as B'nai Synagogue, meaning "Sons of Israel" in Hebrew, the Cubs Den Team Store now occupies this historic space. A plaque at the entrance memorializes the 1901 Romanesque Revival-style building. Designed by South Bend architects Freyemuth and Maurer, it was the first Jewish place of worship in the area. After serving an active congregation for over 90 years, the building was transferred to Indiana Landmarks. A significant $1 million renovation transformed it into a team store, and in 2013, it earned a prestigious spot on the National Register of Historic Places.

Inside are unexpected sights that deviate from a typical team store. The building still contains stained-glass windows, a chandelier suspended from the ceiling, and a refurbished bimah. Inside a doorway, words from Exodus are scripted across the wall, "Make for me a sanctuary, and I will dwell in their midst."

Photo courtesy of South Bend Cubs

CUBS DEN TEAM STORE

WHAT: A minor-league baseball team store inside a former synagogue

WHERE: 420 S William St., South Bend

COST: Free to visit

PRO TIP: Adjacent to Four Winds Field, the South Bend Cubs Team Store offers parking for customers and is conveniently within walking distance for game attendees.

Photos courtesy of South Bend Cubs

A reproduction of Michelangelo's *Creation of Adam* hangs behind the cash register, stirring mixed emotions among visitors. Some may find the depiction of Adam reaching out with a baseball glove jarring, while others appreciate the restoration efforts that have brought the building back to life.

Team owner and Chicago Cubs minority owner Andrew Berlin describes himself as a "twice-a-year Jew" and had an Old Testament verse on a plaque displayed within the building, adding a spiritual element to the space.

Similar to the historic rooftop ads situated beyond the left field wall of Wrigley Field, the Cubs Den features a Toyota advertisement prominently displayed across its roof.

WHITEWATER RAFTING IN THE CITY

Where is the nation's first artificial whitewater rafting course?

An unexpected gem awaits in the heart of downtown South Bend, Indiana—whitewater rafting. As a former resident of the northern Indiana region, I've had the privilege of experiencing the East Race Waterway. Still, I'm continually amazed by the number of people who have yet to learn of this hidden treasure. This unique urban adventure deserves a spot in this book, offering a thrilling contrast to the city's traditional attractions. Before transforming into a whitewater rafting course, this waterway was part of a former hydroelectric factory and left vacant as a trash heap. The construction of this remarkable course took two years and $5 million, resulting in an exhilarating rafting experience.

Since opening in 1984, East Race Waterway has welcomed nearly half a million rafters.

From June to September, thrill-seekers and whitewater rafting enthusiasts can venture into downtown South Bend on weekends to experience the nation's first man-made whitewater rafting course. Despite not being the Colorado River, this outdoor course offers an exciting adventure in Indiana. With a length of 2,000 feet and a total fall of around 12 feet, depending on the river's flow, the course features rapids that can generate waves up to six feet or higher.

A ride takes approximately five minutes and is accessible to individuals over 54 inches tall (no experience required). Kayaks are also permitted and accessible on the East Race Waterway, providing an alternative paddling option for those who prefer not to share a raft.

EAST RACE WATERWAY

WHAT: An outdoor whitewater course in the city

WHERE: 126 S Niles Ave., South Bend

COST: Free for admission

PRO TIP: Book your trip online in advance. They offer one to three rides and all-day passes.

AN ELEPHANT IN THE SHOP

How did a 1,200-pound elephant end up crashing through the doors of a drugstore?

In 1942, the Great American Circus arrived in Wabash, Indiana. The circus owner, Lyman Keyes, announced that the November 11 performance would be their last until the end of World War II because many circus hands were called to serve in the war.

Three female elephants, July, Empress, and Modoc, were part of the circus act. They waited outside the Wabash High School gym, tethered and ready for their performance. However, a group of barking dogs startled all three elephants, causing them to break free from their tethers. Empress and July wandered nearby and were recaptured. Modoc had a different plan—she bolted away, eager for an unexpected adventure.

MODOC'S MARKET

WHAT: A coffee shop with an iconic story

WHERE: 205 S Miami St., Wabash

COST: Varies (budget-friendly)

PRO TIP: This is a great spot for hanging out, with free Wi-Fi, lots of seating, and a children's area.

The 1,200-pound Modoc was drawn to the enticing aroma of roasted peanuts from the Bradley Brothers Drugstore in downtown Wabash. The drugstore was surprised when Modoc charged in, knocking over a customer and toppling the peanut roaster. The elephant's

---

Modoc's Market is in the Wabash Downtown Historic District, recognized by the National Register of Historic Places and the Historic Landmarks Foundation of Indiana.

adventure continued for five days, making national headline news. Eventually, Modoc's rampage was halted when she was lured back with 26 loaves of bread and six quarts of whiskey to soothe her frazzled nerves.

The Brady Brothers Drugstore is now known as Modoc's Market. Outside, an elephant statue stands, and inside the market, visitors can read the fascinating story of Modoc. Modoc's Market is a small market, gift shop, café, and espresso bar. Step inside, and you can order one of their "elephant drinks," a tribute to the market's namesake.

Garden of Gas Station Signs

SOURCES

An Open-Air Utopian Sanctuary
Atlas Obscura. "The Roofless Church." www.atlasobscura.com/places/the-roofless-church-new-harmony-indiana
Robert Lee Blaffer Foundation. "Experience JBO Sanctuary." www.robertleeblafferfoundation.org/home/blaffer-sanctuary-features

A Library with Secrets within the Books
French Lick Resort. "Notes From the Past, Hiding in West Baden Springs Hotel Library." www.frenchlickresort.blogspot.com/2022/04/notes-from-past-hiding-in-west-baden.

Otis the Sasquatch
Johnson, Carol. "'Otis,' the Orange County Sasquatch Sensation." *Limestone Post*, May 24, 2024. https://limestonepostmagazine.com/otis-orange-county-sasquatch-sensation/

A Taste from Outer Space
Shadburne, Sarah. "Visit this sci-fi diner in New Albany, IN." *LOU Today*, July 15, 2022, https://loutoday.6amcity.com/visit-this-sci-fi-diner-in-new-albany-in.

The Official Train Robbers
Atlas Obscura. "Graves of the Reno Gang." https://www.atlasobscura.com/places/graves-of-the-reno-gang
Henson, Janet. "Reno Gang Graves," *Discover Indiana*, August 21, 2021, https://discoverindianahistory.org/items/show/598

A Pioneer's Legacy
Beck's Mill. "History." https://becksmill.org/

Shade for Indiana's Founding Fathers
Indiana State Museum. "Preserving the Constitution Elm." https://indianastatemuseum.wordpress.com/2012/11/07/preserving-the-constitution-elm/

A Bookstore with a Secret Tunnel
Indiana Humanities. "Your Brother's Bookstore: Tunnel Story." https://youtu.be/RvYH6alp8mk?si=05hT45Db-RiNNIYD

The Grey Lady in the Library
Willard Public Library. "About Us." www.willard.lib.in.us/about-us

Burger Bar inside a Bus Terminal
Indiana Landmarks. "A Reason to Linger." https://www.indianalandmarks.org/2016/09/bru-burger-construction-evansville-greyhound/

The House of Doctors
Ferdinand Historical Society. "Historic Wollenmann House." http://ferdinandhistory.org/

A Timepiece with Buried Secrets
Rickert, A. (2023, September 8). Historians researching possible burial site at the former Colgate property in Clarksville. *Louisville Public Media*. https://www.lpm.org/news/2023-09-08/historians-researching-possible-burial-site-at-the-former-colgate-property-in-clarksville

A Wildcat Story
Fairview Elementary. "History of Fairview Elementary School." https://fairview.mccsc.edu/

World's Longest Trestle Bridge
Tulip Trestle Community Restoration, Inc. "Home." https://www.tuliptrestle.org/

A Grotto Built from Geodes
Rutter, K. (2020, June 11). Jasper's Geode Grotto offers visitors beauty, peace, place to pray. The Message, *Southwestern Indiana's Catholic Community Newspaper*. https://evdiomessage.org/jaspers-geode-grotto-offers-visitors-beauty-peace-place-to-pray/

A Hardware Store Time Capsule
Crane, M. (2020, May 18). Sturm Hardware: The Living Museum. *Dubois County Free Press, Inc.* https://duboiscountyfreepress.com/sturms-the-living-museum/

The Only Operational Rotary Jail in the Country
The Indiana Historical Bureau. *The Indiana Historian*. "Montgomery County Jail Machine." Indianapolis, October 1994.

The *Ben-Hur* Study
General Lew Wallace Study & Museum. "Study Building." https://www.ben-hur.com/about-us/study-building/

A TV Star's Nonprofit Arcade
Rupert's Kids. "About Rupert." https://www.rupertskids.org/about-rupert

An Italian POW Chapel
Indiana Historical Society. *INDepth Stories*. "You Are There 1943: Italian POWs at Atterbury." https://indianahistory.org/stories/you-are-there-1943-italian-pows-at-atterbury/
Italian Heritage Society of Indiana. "Italian P.O.W. Chapel of Our Lady in the Meadow." https://italianheritage.org/about/italian-p-o-w-chapel-lady-meadow/

A Japanese Oasis
Trares, R. (2023, October 10). Immersive mural experience coming to Franklin's Kuji Alley. *Daily Journal*, Franklin, Indiana.

A Garden of Vintage Gas Station Signs
Pemberton, M. (2019, July 24). "Whiteland's 'Sign Guy' has a new glowing restoration." *Indy Star*, Indianapolis.
Roadside America. "Whiteland, Indiana: Garden of Gas Station Signs." https://www.roadsideamerica.com/tip/48609

The Home Where Little Orphan Annie Lived
Van Allen, Elizabeth J. *James Whitcomb Riley: A Life*. Indiana University Press, Bloomington and Indianapolis, 1999.

A Railroad Treasure Trove
Monon Connection. "Museum." https://mononconnection.net

A World Record-Holding Ball
Atlas Obscura. "World's Largest Ball of Paint." https://www.atlasobscura.com/places/worlds-largest-ball-of-paint

One School in Two States
The Union School 1893-2004 Ohio Historical Marker. College Corner in Preble County, Ohio. Marker Number 5-68.

The Couple Buried in a State Park
"Lieber Dies of Heart Seizure." *Journal and Courier*, Lafayette, Indiana, April 17, 1944, p. 5.

Indiana State University Library. *Shadows of the Washash–ISU Special Collections*. "Old Log Church." www.indstate.contentdm.oclc.org/digital/collection/isulib/id/2435

Outlaws and Artifacts
Hamilton County Historical Society. "At the Museum." https://www.hamiltoncoinhs.com/

New York City's First Skyscraper in a Park
Friends of Holliday Park. Resources. "History of the Ruins at Holliday Park." https://www.hollidaypark.org/resources/Ruins.pdf

Coffee in a Former Mental Hospital
Saenz, E. (2024, January 1). Westside coffee shop offers a taste of the timeless—and maybe a ghost. *Mirror Indy*.

The Building with Brains
Indiana Medical History Museum. "About Us." https://www.imhm.org/about/
Giorgio, Mary. "The Unsolved Murder of Dr. Helen Knabe." Orange Bean Indiana, 13 Sept. 2019, https://orangebeanindiana.com/2019/09/13/the-unsolved-murder-of-dr-helen-knabe/

A Rock-and-Roll Time Capsule
Atlas Obscura. "Elvis Presley Final Concert Plaque." https://www.atlasobscura.com/places/elvis-presley-final-concert-indianapolis
Lindquist, D. (2018, June 26). You can now find Elvis Presley's final concert plaque amid shiny new spots on Market Street. *Indy Star*, Indianapolis.

A Cycling Stadium
Indy Cycloplex. "Track." https://indycycloplex.com/track

The Tuberculosis Hospital
The Sanatorium. "Indiana State Sanatorium." https://thesanatorium.net/

A Real-Life Mayberry Experience
Mayberry Cafe. "About." https://www.mayberrycafe.com/

A Periodic-Table Museum
Theodore Gray. "Periodic Table." https://theodoregray.com/PeriodicTable/

A Church Adorned with Tiffany Glass
The Reid Center. "About Us." https://www.reidcenter.org/about
Indiana Landmarks. "Reid Memorial Presbyterian Church." https://www.indianalandmarks.org/endangered-property/reid-memorial-presbyterian-church/

A Walk among Legends
Starr-Gennett Foundation. "Walk of Fame Medallions." https://www.starrgennettfoundation.org/gennett-records-wof

A Fountain from Brazil
Indiana Landmarks. "Western Indiana's Brazilian Landmark." https://www.indianalandmarks.org/2016/06/western-indianas-brazilian-landmark/
Clay County Parks. "Our Mission." https://claycountyparks.org/what-we-do

An Eight-Sided House
Reeves Octagon House. "About the Octagon House." https://reevesoctagonhouse.com/about-the-octagon-house-history/

A Tree-Mendous Courthouse Curiosity
Visit Greensburg. "World Famous Tower Tree." https://www.visitgreensburg.com/tower-tree/

Courthouse with a *Star Trek* Connection
United States Department of the Interior, National Park Service. (n.d.). National Register of Historic Places Inventory-Nomination Form for Boone County Courthouse. https://secure.in.gov/apps/dnr/shaard/r/1fd97/N/Boone_CO_Courthouse_Nom.pdf

Wonders of the Night Sky
Prairie Grass Observatory. "Prairie Grass Observatory." https://indianastars.com/

Indiana's Sleepy Hollow
Willis, W. L. (2015, April 7). Sleepy Hollow. America's Haunted Road Trip. http://americashauntedroadtrip.com/sleepy-hollow/

Vault Dining Experience
Crame, M. (2024, September 9). "Butcher and Barrel redeFINING dining." *Dubois County Free Press*, Huntingburg

The Goldfish Capital of the World
Ozark Fisheries. "Ozark Fisheries History." https://www.ozarkfisheries.com/pages/our-history

A Footwear Fortress
Lost Indiana. "International Palace of Sports (North Webster)." https://lostindiana.net/2009/08/01/international-palace-of-sports-north-webster/

The Legacy of Lake Webster
Ride the Dixie. "History." http://www.ridethedixie.com/

A Slice of Horror
Famous Monster Pizza. "About Us." https://www.famousmonsterpizza.com/about-us

An Excavated Sunken Oasis
City of Huntington, IN. Locations. "Sunken Gardens." https://www.huntington.in.us/egov/apps/locations/facilities.egov

A Stuffed Dog from 1900
Find A Grave. Memorials. "Old Sully." https://www.findagrave.com/memorial/259990720/old_sully

A Canal with Irish Heritage
Fatout, Paul (1972). *Indiana Canals*. Purdue University Press.
Visit Wabash County, Indiana. "Canal Played Major Factor in Developing Wabash County." https://www.visitwabashcounty.com/stories/canal-played-major-factor-in-developing-wabash-county/

Splinters from the Cross
Schmitz, Mariam. "Cathedral Museum Highlights Church and Diocesan History." *Today's Catholic*, Fort Wayne, January 2, 2018. https://todayscatholic.org/cathedral-museum-highlights-church-diocesan-history/

Indiana's "Grand Canyon"
The Waynedale News.com. "Watch for Quarry Observation Tower Upgrades." https://waynedalenews.com/2023/11/watch-for-quarry-tower-upgrades/

Letters from Lincoln
Friends of the Lincoln Collections. "The Rolland Center." https://www.friendsofthelincolncollection.org/the-rolland-center/

Monster-Truck Mania
International Monster Truck Museum. "About The Museum." https://monstermuseum.org/

A Sanctuary of Healing through Water
Lourdes Grotto. "Rome City, IN: Kneipp Springs Sanitarium." https://lourdesgrottos.com/2023/06/03/rome-city-in-kneipp-springs-sanitarium/

A Treasure Trove of American Art
Midwest Museum of American Art. "Collection." https://www.midwestmuseum.org/

Behind-the-Curtain Tour
The Lerner. "Experience a Guided Tour." https://thelerner.com/plan-your-visit/tour-the-lerner/

The RV and Trailer Capital of the World
Inside Indiana Business. "How Elkhart Became the RV Capital of the World." https://www.insideindianabusiness.com/articles/thursday-how-elkhart-became-the-RV-capital-of-the-world

The Submarine Secrets of Lake Michigan
Harris, Patricia A. Gruse. "The Great Lakes' First Submarine L.D. Phillips' Fool Killer." *Inland Seas*, Fall 1983, https://nmgl.org/the-great-lakes-first-submarine-ld-phillips-fool-killer-fall-1983/

The Solitary Columns
Cannon, Thomas H., H. H. Loring, and Charles J. Robb. 1927. *History of the Lake and Calumet Region of Indiana, Embracing the Counties of Lake, Porter and LaPorte: An Historical Account of Its People and Its Progress from the Earliest Times to the Present. Volume I.* Indianapolis, Indiana: Historians' Association. 840 p. https://www.inportercounty.org/Data/Misc/PorterCountyHistory-1927/PorterCountyHistory-1927-Chapter24.html

The "Poor Man's Harvard" Chapel
Valparaiso University. "History." https://www.valpo.edu/about/history/

A Ferris-Wheel Tale
The Historical Marker Database. "Legendary Dunn's Bridge." https://www.hmdb.org/m.asp?m=210346
Porter County Park. "Dunn's Bridge County Park." Ihttps://www.portercountyparks.org/dunns-bridge

Echoes of the Past
Lake County Parks & Rec. "Buckley Homestead." https://lakecountyparks.com/149/Buckley-Homestead

The Mass-Produced Marvel
City of Kokomo. "Elwood Haynes Museum." https://www.cityofkokomo.org/departments/elwood_haynes_museum.php

Where Fiction Meets Snacks
American Dirt. "Reviving with the wave of a wizard's wand." https://dirtamericana.com/2013/01/storybook-reviving-wave-wizards-wand/
Fortune Companies, Inc. "Storybook Express." https://fc-inc.com/projects/storybook-express

The Preserved Pair
City of Kokomo. "Sycamore Stump." https://www.cityofkokomo.org/departments/sycamore_stump.php
Visit Kokomo. "Old Ben - World's Largest Steer." https://visitkokomo.org/search-kokomo/old-ben-worlds-largest-steer/

The Big-Top Legacy

International Circus Hall of Fame. https://circushalloffame.com/visiting-the-ichof/

Peru Amateur Circus. "Circus City Museum." https://www.perucircus.com/museum

Pillars of Time

Miami Indians. "Seven Pillars." https://www.miamiindians.org/seven-pillars

Orange Bean. "Seven Pillars of the Mississinewa." https://orangebeanindiana.com/2019/12/05/seven-pillars-of-the-mississinewa/

The Cabin within a House

Tilcor Roofing Systems. "Tilcor Chosen For Historic Roof Restoration–Blann Log Cabin." https://www.tilcor.com/us/news-blogs/tilcor-chosen-for-historic-roof-restoration-blann-log-cabin/

Visit Newton County. "Historic County Cabin–Newton County's Oldest Structure." https://visitnewtoncountyin.com/places-to-go/

An Intergalactic Voyage

Purdue Alumnus. "Cosmetic Connection." https://www.purduealumnus.org/cosmic-connection/campus/

The Gas Station Transformation

Purdue University. (n.d.). Red-Crown Mini Museum. Retrieved March 25, 2020, from http://www.oldgas.com/info/redcrown.htm

Wall of Murals

The Arts Federation. "Wabash Walls." https://wabashwalls.theartsfederation.org/

The Whispering Windmills

Mid-American Windmill Museum. "About Us." https://www.midamericawindmillmuseum.org/about

Worship on the Water

Keh, Andrew. "A House of Worship, Converted." *New York Times*, New York, May 26, 2015.

The Unlikely Home of a Team Store

Connor, T. (2020). *Indiana Landmarks: Rescued & Restored*. Indiana Landmarks.

Whitewater Rafting in the City

WTHR 13. "Rafting along the East Race Waterway." YouTube, 2023, https://youtu.be/InjCP-fgtq8?si=_OUDT4NdpOo88gNV

An Elephant in the Shop

Modoc's Market. "The Story of Modoc the Elephant." https://www.modocsmarket.com/the-story-of-modoc.html

INDEX

The Lerner Theatre

Geode Grotto